AF352012

# Money
## Adventure
**YOUR GUIDE TO FINANCIAL FREEDOM**

———

AARON B KERSHAW

# Copyright

**Money Adventure**
Cover design, editing, and layout.
By Aaron B.  Kershaw
Language: English
Publication Date: 2024
Format: eBook, Paperback

# Table of Contents

VIII

IX

# INTRODUCTION

## Welcome to Uncle Aaron's Money Adventure

Hey there, welcome to Money Adventure! I'm Uncle Aaron, and trust me, this is not your average, snooze-worthy financial guide. I've been through it all—from getting my first paycheck in the Marines and thinking I was rich, to learning the hard way just how quickly money can slip through your fingers if you don't have a plan.

Let me give you a little background. Yep, I'm a proud veteran of the U.S. Marines, where I learned how to be disciplined and how to make do with not much (believe me, I've eaten more canned beans than I'd like to admit). After my military days, I dove headfirst into the business world—starting companies, making investments, and figuring out how to make money work for me instead of the other way around. I've had some solid wins, but I've also hit my fair share of bumps along the way—just ask my first side hustle (spoiler alert: it was a hot mess). I'm here to pass on what I've learned so you don't have to make the same mistakes.

**Now, I know what you're thinking:** "Another boring money book? Hard pass." But hang on a sec! This isn't a dry lecture filled with jargon that makes your eyes glaze over. We're keeping it real, practical, and we're going to have some fun along the way. The truth is, managing money doesn't have to be hard—it just has to make sense.

## Why Money Matters for You

**Here's the deal:** Financial literacy is essential, whether you're just getting your first paycheck or trying to escape a paycheck-to-paycheck cycle. The sooner you understand how money works, the sooner you can make it work for you. Maybe you're tired of stressing about bills, or maybe you dream of ditching the 9-to-5 for something that gives you more freedom. Either way, knowing how to handle money is the key to unlocking options in life—freedom to make choices, to take risks, and to build the future you want.

I'm here to show you how to budget without losing your mind, save for what really matters, and set yourself up for long-term success—without feeling like you're stuck living off ramen noodles. We'll tackle everything from making your paycheck last longer than your weekend to building wealth without needing a six-figure salary. And when life inevitably throws you a curveball (because it will), I'll teach you how to dodge it like a pro.

## My "Aha!" Moment

I'll never forget the day I had my own financial wake-up call. Fresh out of the Marines, I thought I had money all figured out. I mean, I was disciplined, right? But then, one day, after a particularly indulgent weekend (hello, new stereo system and takeout galore), I checked my bank balance and got hit with a cold dose of reality. Let's just say that overdraft fees are a cruel teacher. That's when I realized: if I didn't learn to manage my money, my money was going to manage me—and not in a fun way.

That was my "aha" moment. From that day forward, I promised myself I'd get smart about finances, and I've been on that journey ever since. Now, I want to help you get there without those "oops" moments along the way.

## What You'll Learn

*(And Why You Should Care)*

Whether you're just starting out, juggling multiple jobs, or trying to turn your side hustle into a serious business, I've got your back. We'll go over:

- How to make your paycheck stretch without feeling deprived.

- Building wealth even if you don't have a fancy job title or a six-figure salary.
- Protecting yourself from financial disasters—because life loves to throw those when you least expect it.
- And, most importantly, how to make money feel less stressful and more manageable.

**Ready to Get Started?**

So, buckle up! We're about to start a journey that'll help you take control of your finances and, ultimately, your life. This is your adventure, and I'm here to guide you every step of the way. Trust me, it's going to be worth it—and maybe even a little fun.

**Ready to join me on this adventure? Let's do this!**

# PART 1:

*Financial Foundations*

## BLUEPRINT FOR BUILDING YOUR MONEY HOUSE
*(Without Using Duct Tape)*

Welcome to the foundation of your financial adventure! Think of this part as the bedrock of your money house—you can't build a mansion on sand, right? We're laying down the solid ground rules that will keep your financial life steady, secure, and ready for whatever life throws your way. Forget the flimsy quick-fix solutions; we're talking bricks, not Band-Aids.

**Here's the thing:** like many of you, I didn't grow up with that crucial foundational knowledge about money. It wasn't until well into my 40's that I finally had the level of understanding needed to find real success and security in life. And let me tell you, it doesn't have to take that long. My goal with this book is to fast-track your financial education, so you don't have to spend years figuring it out the hard way like I did. Whether you've been winging it or just getting by, that ends now.

In this section, we're covering the essentials: from understanding how money works (and why it always seems to slip through your fingers) to mastering the psychology behind it—because half the battle is getting your head in the right place. By the end of this part, you'll have the tools to start budgeting like a pro and saving for the fun stuff and the unexpected.

Ready to pour a rock-solid financial foundation?

**Grab your hard hat—let's get building!**

# 1

# <u>Understanding Money</u><br><u>&</u><br><u>How It Works</u>

Alright, gather 'round, folks! Let's talk about money—yeah, you heard me. The thing we never seem to have enough of, but that somehow controls so much of our lives. Now, before you go rolling your eyes and thinking, "Here we go, another boring 'be responsible with your money' lecture," trust me, Uncle Aaron's got you covered.

We're going to break this down in a way that makes sense to you today. And yes, I'll throw in some stories of how I learned these lessons the hard way—because spoiler alert: I didn't always have it together.

## WHAT IS MONEY, REALLY?

So, what is money? At its core, money is just a tool—a way to exchange value. It's what lets you pay rent, buy that slick new pair of sneakers, or hit up your favorite coffee spot for an overpriced cappuccino.

**Here's the kicker:** money isn't just something you spend. It's something you need to understand, respect, and control. Otherwise, it'll control you—and trust me, that's a wild ride you don't want to take.

**Now, back in the** day—I'm talking about the '90s here—money looked a little different. We didn't have Venmo, Pay-Pal, or Bitcoin wallets. Nope, it was cash or the good ol' checkbook. And if you were feeling fancy, you had a debit card that you prayed wouldn't get declined. And don't even get me started on Pay-Per-View—where you'd pay to watch that big boxing match or rent a movie if you didn't feel like hitting up Blockbuster.

And here's a fun fact—Netflix? Not even a thing yet. We had cable, VHS tapes, and if you were lucky, premium channels like HBO, which was the holy grail for movie nights.

## STORY TIME WITH UNCLE AARON: THE $400 PIZZA

I'll never forget the time I learned a hard lesson about money—fresh out of the Marines, about 22 years old. I thought I had this money thing all figured out. I'd just gotten my first job after leaving the Corps and felt like I had the world at my feet.

**So, one Friday ni**ght, I decided to treat myself to a pizza—you know, because obviously, I deserved it after a week of pretending I knew what I was doing at my new job.

Now, this wasn't just any pizza. Oh no. It was a $25 deep-dish special from the best spot in town. I didn't have a ton of money, but I figured, "Hey, I worked hard, I deserve this." I called it in, paid with my trusty debit card, grabbed a six-pack, and settled down for a movie on Pay-Per-View—probably some action flick with more explosions than plot.

**Fast forward to Monday morning**—I'm feeling good, ready to tackle the week, and I decide to check my bank account. And boom—there it was. I got hit with a $35 overdraft fee.

Apparently, I had less in my account than I thought, and that pizza (plus the six-pack and movie) ended up costing me over $400 by the time the overdraft snowball finished rolling.

**Lesson learned?**

Always know what's in your account, and don't spend money you don't have. I thought I was treating myself, but I ended up in a financial hole for a pizza and a night in. Trust me, pizza should never cost that much.

## MONEY IS A FLOW, NOT JUST A DESTINATION

**Here's something you need to understand about money:** it's not just something you save or something you spend.

**It's a flow.** Picture it like a river—money comes in (from your job, side hustles, or that birthday check from Grandma), and money flows out (to bills, savings, and yes, fun stuff like pizza or concert tickets).

If you don't know how to manage that flow, you're either going to end up drowning in debt or bone dry. That's why some people with modest salaries can live comfortably—they've mastered the flow. Meanwhile, you've got folks making six figures who are living paycheck to paycheck because they let the current sweep them away.

## COMPOUND INTEREST: YOUR BEST FRIEND
*(Or Worst Enemy)*

Now let's get into something that'll either be your best friend or your worst enemy: compound interest. If you're saving money or investing it, compound interest is a gift that keeps on giving. It's like a snowball rolling down a hill—it starts small, but as it keeps rolling, it gets bigger and bigger. And before you know it, you've got a giant snowball of money working for you.

But here's the flip side—if you're racking up credit card debt or ignoring those student loans, compound interest becomes your enemy real fast. Every month you don't pay it off, it's like you're rolling that snowball in the wrong direction, and it's gaining size at your expense.

## BACK IN MY DAY:
*How Things Have Changed*

Let me tell you—back in my day, managing money wasn't this "tap your phone and transfer money instantly" deal. We didn't have apps that tracked every latte you bought or helped you invest spare change.

Nope, it was manual. You wrote checks, you logged things in a little register, and you hoped the check didn't bounce.

Things have changed, but the fundamentals are still the same. Whether you're using cash, plastic, or digital currency, the key is knowing how it works and how it flows.

Money represents value—and while it's easy to spend it, keeping it and making it grow? That's a whole different ball game.

## TYPES OF MONEY
*Cash, Credit, and Crypto*

Alright, let's dig a little deeper into the different forms of money floating around today. While cash is still king in some situations, we've got a lot more options these days.

### *CASH*

You've probably used this one since you were a kid. Cash is

tangible, easy to spend, but just as easy to lose. It's great for face-to-face transactions, but once it's gone, it's gone.

**1.** Credit

Credit cards are a whole different ball game. It's like spending money that isn't yours—yet.

When used responsibly, credit can be your friend (think of those travel points!), but if you're not careful, you'll find yourself paying for that pizza for years.

**Fun fact: Did you** know Uncle Aaron once tried to buy concert tickets and a stereo on a credit card? Yeah, ended up paying twice the price in interest. *LESSON LEARNED!*

## DIGITAL CURRENCY
*(Crypto)*

Then there's cryptocurrency—the new kid on the block. It's digital, decentralized, and doesn't live in a physical wallet. It's still gaining ground, and unless you're deep in the tech game, you probably aren't using it to pay for everyday things just yet.

That said, crypto is becoming more popular, so keep an eye on it. I tried paying for my coffee with Bitcoin once—let's just say, the barista wasn't ready for that yet.

## INFLATION:
*The Sneaky Erosion of Your Cash*

Now, let's dive into something called inflation. Inflation is the reason your grandparents can go on and on about how they used to pay a nickel for a Coke and why you're now paying $2.50 for the same thing.

Inflation is like a stealthy little gremlin that sneaks in over time, making everything cost more. What was once cheap is now expensive, and it doesn't just apply to soda.

**Here's how it works:** As time goes by, the value of money decreases, and the cost of things like groceries, gas, and rent increases. This is inflation at play. It's the reason why if you stuff $1,000 under your mattress for 20 years, it'll buy you less than it would have today. You might have $1,000, but what you can buy with it has shrunk—kind of like your favorite shirt after one too many trips through the dryer.

## INTEREST: THE GOOD, THE BAD, AND THE UGLY

Now, let's talk interest—your best friend when you're saving, but your worst enemy when you're in debt. Interest is how banks and credit cards either reward you or punish you depending on whether you're borrowing or saving.

### *Good Interest: Compound Interest*

Let's start with the good side—compound interest is like free money making babies. It's the magic that turns a small investment into a large one over time. If you save or invest, compound interest will make your money grow without you lifting a finger.

For example, if you invest $1,000 today at a 7% annual interest rate, in 10 years, you'll have almost $2,000 without adding a single penny more!

### *Bad Interest: Debt*

On the flip side, if you're carrying debt, interest becomes your enemy. The longer you wait to pay off debt, the bigger it gets, thanks to the same principle of compounding—only now, it's working against you.

Credit card interest is particularly nasty, and if you don't pay off your balance, you'll end up paying way more than you originally borrowed.

That's why that $100 pair of shoes can easily end up costing you $200 or more over time if you only make the minimum payments.

## KEY TAKEAWAYS:

2. **Know where your money is:** Keep track of what's coming in and what's going out. Don't end up like me with a $400 pizza story.
3. **Respect the flow:** Think of money like a river—manage it, or it'll manage you. And don't let it sweep you away.
4. **Embrace compound interest:** It's either your greatest ally in building wealth or your worst enemy when it comes to debt.
5. **Understand the types of money:** Cash, credit, and crypto all work differently. Learn how to manage each so you're never caught off guard.
6. **Handle interest carefully:** Compound interest can make you rich if you invest, but it can also ruin you if you're in debt.

## WHAT WE COVERED:

We dove into what money really is (not just something you spend on lattes), inflation, compound interest, and why it's important to start thinking about money now—before life throws you a curveball.

### WHAT I WANT YOU TO REMEMBER:

**Money is a tool.** *It's not just about getting through this month's bills, it's about playing the long game. Start using compound interest to your advantage, and don't let inflation sneak up on you.*

Trust me, future-you will thank you!

## UNCLE AARON'S ACTION PLAN

◊ **Track Your Spending:** Start writing down every dollar you spend for one week.

◊ **Open a High-Yield Savings Account:** If your savings aren't growing, you're losing money to inflation.

◊ **Set a Small Savings Goal:** Save just $50 this month and see how good it feels.

# 2

# MASTERING THE PSYCHOLOGY OF MONEY

## HOW EMOTIONS INFLUENCE YOUR FINANCES

*The Emotional Side of Money*

My nephew, nick-named "Zero", has been killing it in the influencer world. At just 26, he's built a career as a professional photographer and social media influencer, jet-setting between Miami's beaches and some of the world's most exclusive destinations. His brand deals come with big paychecks, and his Instagram feed is the definition of #Goals. But even with all his success, Zero knows that managing money can sometimes feel like an emotional roller-coaster.

It wasn't always that way. Zero didn't start with flashy gear or endless opportunities. I remember the day I handed him his first professional camera—the same one I started my own career with. I had it refurbished, polished, and made sure it was in perfect working order. *"This camera has seen it all,"* I told him. *"It's taken me places I never thought I'd go. Now, it's yours to carry you forward."* Zero's eyes lit up as he held the camera, knowing it represented more than just a piece of equipment—it was the start of his professional journey.

For years, Zero worked magic with that camera. He learned every button, every setting, and produced stunning shots that put him on the map. But as his career grew, so did his ambitions. He started eyeing the newer models, ones with higher megapixels, better video capabilities, and of course, more appeal in the influencer space. The day came when Zero decided to upgrade to a brand-new, top-of-the-line camera. I wasn't surprised, but I could tell there were mixed emotions involved.

On one hand, Zero was excited—he was at a point in his career where upgrading made sense. He'd saved up, worked hard, and earned the right to invest in better tools. But on the other hand, he felt a pang of guilt. That old camera had been with him through thick and thin, and letting it go wasn't just about parting with a piece of equipment—it felt like closing a chapter on the early days of his career. *"It's tough,"* he said. *"This new camera is amazing, but I can't shake the feeling that I'm betraying the one that got me here."*

Even in moments of success, emotions like nostalgia and attachment can play a huge role in financial decisions. **Zero's story highlights a core truth:** No matter how logical or well-thought-out a purchase is, our feelings have a way of sneaking into the equation.

## THE SCIENCE BEHIND MONEY AND EMOTIONS

Turns out, Zero isn't the only one who's ever felt torn between upgrading and holding onto something with sentimental value. There's a whole field of science that explains why we sometimes let our emotions run the show when it comes to money. It's called Behavioral Finance, and it looks at how psychology influences our financial choices.

Take something called Loss Aversion, for example. This is the idea that people tend to fear losing money or parting with something valuable more than they enjoy gaining something new. It's why Zero hesitated when upgrading his camera—because part of him didn't want to **"lose"** the attachment to the old one, even though the new camera was a better fit for his career. I've seen it in Uncle Aaron, too—he's the kind of guy who'll hold onto a pair of shoes long past their prime because he hates the idea of getting rid of something he's invested in.

Then there's *Anchoring*, a psychological bias where people rely too heavily on the first piece of information they get when making decisions. For Zero, his old camera was the anchor. It was the benchmark against which he judged all other equipment. So even when the new models came out, he kept thinking, *"Does it really outshine the one that got me started?"*

## FOMO: FEAR OF MISSING OUT

And then, of course, there's FOMO—Fear of Missing Out. In case you're wondering, FOMO is that feeling you get when you see others doing something or buying something, and suddenly you feel like you need to do the same, just so you don't get left behind. For Zero, FOMO often crept in during his social media scrolls. When you're an influencer, it's hard not to compare yourself to others in the industry. Seeing fellow photographers with the latest gear or heading off to exotic shoots can make you question whether you're doing enough—even when you're already on the top of your game.

*"I see other photographers with all this new gear,"* Zero said one day. *"And it makes me think, 'Should I be upgrading? Should I be investing in even more equipment?'"* That's the tricky thing with FOMO—it can make you second-guess your own progress,

pushing you to spend money just to keep up, even when it's not necessary.

Uncle Aaron, of course, has his own version of FOMO. It's not camera gear or tropical vacations that get him—it's his neighbors. Every time Bob next door gets something new, like a grill with all the bells and whistles or a car that's fresher than his, Uncle Aaron starts thinking, *"Maybe it's time for an upgrade."* Next thing you know, he's back from the store with a lawnmower that practically drives itself.

## COMMON EMOTIONAL TRIGGERS IN FINANCIAL DECISION-MAKING

Zero and Uncle Aaron might be at different stages in their careers, but the emotional triggers that influence their financial decisions are surprisingly similar.

For Zero, it's all about managing the uncertainty of freelance life. Being a photographer and influencer means that his income can fluctuate, and that unpredictably creates a lot of anxiety. Some months, he's flush with cash from brand deals and international gigs. Other months, the work slows down, and the anxiety starts creeping in. That's when he's tempted to either overwork—taking on too many projects or under-spend, worrying that the success won't last. Even with his success, there's always that lingering fear that the next big gig might not come.

Uncle Aaron, on the other hand, grew up in a time when money was tight, and that's left its mark. He's the definition of a Scarcity Mindset—always saving, always cautious, sometimes to a fault. *"I remember the days when we had to pinch every penny,"* he says. "That sticks with you, even when you're doing well. It's hard to shake the feeling that it could all disappear tomorrow."

Zero, being the savvy guy he is, recognizes these emotional

triggers, both in himself and in Uncle Aaron. He knows that managing his mindset is key to making smart financial decisions—especially when it comes to investing in his career and planning for the future.

## MANAGING YOUR MONEY MINDSET

Now, don't get me wrong—Zero's good with his money. He didn't get to where he is by being reckless. But like anyone, even Zero could benefit from managing the emotional side of his finances.

One thing he's learned over the years is the power of automation. After landing a few big deals, Zero decided to set up automatic transfers to a **"future studio fund."** Every month, a portion of his income goes straight into savings, no matter what. It's his way of making sure that even when the excitement of a new gig or a successful shoot wears off, his long-term goals are still being taken care of.

Then there's the 24-hour rule—something he adopted after one too many impulse buys. Before purchasing anything big, whether it's a new camera lens or some fancy editing software, Zero gives himself 24 hours to think it over. If he still wants it the next day, then he'll go for it. But more often than not, he realizes that the urge to buy was just a fleeting moment of excitement.

Uncle Aaron, of course, has his own version of this. Instead of automating with apps, he's more of a "sticky note on the fridge" kind of guy. But hey, it works for him! Every bill gets paid on time, and he never misses a beat.

## SHIFTING FROM A SCARCITY TO AN ABUNDANCE MINDSET

One of the biggest lessons Zero's learned in recent years is how to shift from a scarcity mindset to an abundance mindset.

It wasn't easy at first—when you've hustled to build your career from scratch, it's natural to feel like every dollar has to be guarded. But Zero's come to realize that he's built a solid foundation. The gigs will keep coming, the opportunities will continue to grow, and there's no need to operate from a place of fear.

It's something he's tried to pass on to Uncle Aaron, too. *"You don't have to hold onto everything so tightly,"* he told him one day. *"You've worked hard, saved enough. It's okay to enjoy some of it."* Uncle Aaron, of course, is a little more old-school in his thinking, but he's starting to come around. After all, what's the point of building wealth if you never take the time to enjoy it?

The story of Zero's journey from his first camera (the one I gave him) to his decision to upgrade, all while balancing his emotions and making smarter financial choices, serves as a reminder that mastering the psychology of money is just as important as managing the money itself. And with a little help from Uncle Aaron's old-school wisdom, Zero's figured out how to make it all work.

**WHAT WE COVERED:**

We broke down how your brain messes with your financial decisions—like stress spending, FOMO, and avoiding your bank balance. We also talked about shifting from a scarcity to an abundance mindset and why that's key to financial success.

## What I Want You to Remember:

*Your brain is just as important as your budget. If you can't get your mindset right, your wallet will always be playing catch-up. Control your impulses, identify your financial triggers, and* work toward feeling good about saving.

**Uncle Aaron's Action Plan:**

◊ **Recognize Your Financial Triggers:**
Write down your biggest spending temptations.

◊ **Set a Financial Goal:**
Something small but achievable—like saving $20 this week.

◊ **Practice Gratitude:**
List three things you're grateful for each day to shift into an abundance mindset.

# 3

## BUDGETING LIKE A PRO

Alright, buckle up because we're diving headfirst into the wild, thrilling world of budgeting—yeah, I said it. Now, before you start groaning and thinking this is just another boring "let's be responsible" lecture, trust me, *Uncle Aaron's got you covered.* We're gonna break it down in a way that actually makes sense and doesn't feel like you're being lectured by a spreadsheet.

**Here's the thing:** budgeting doesn't have to suck. In fact, once you get the hang of it, it can be one of your best friends. Think of it like that buddy who always picks you up from the airport, no questions asked, never complains about gas money. Stick with me, and I'll show you how to budget like a pro, Uncle Aaron style.

**Spoiler alert: You might actually enjoy this. Don't say I didn't warn you.**

### WHY BUDGETING MATTERS:
*The Truth No One Wants to Hear*

Let's get real—everyone needs a budget. I don't care if you're working minimum wage, pulling in six figures, or still collecting allowance money from your parents—if you don't have a budget, you're basically playing financial dodgeball with a blindfold on. And trust me, you don't want to get hit in the face with a surprise overdraft fee because you thought that third latte didn't really count.

Back in the '90s, I thought I had it all figured out. Fresh out of the Marines, I'd cash my paycheck on Friday, treat myself to a new CD (yes, kids, CDs), maybe grab some fast food and rent a movie on Pay-Per-View, and by Sunday, I'd be wondering where all my money went. Spoiler alert: it was gone. All of it. Turns out, "winging it" isn't a solid financial strategy.

## THE MAGIC OF AUTOMATION
*Let Technology Do the Work*

Now, before you say, "I'm just bad with money," let me introduce you to your new best friend: automation. Yup, technology is here to save you from yourself.

Remember back in the day when you had to stand in line at the bank to deposit checks or, even worse, mail in bill payments? And if you were really ahead of the game, you'd transfer a few bucks into savings manually—if you even remembered. Well, those were the dark ages, my friend. Today, you've got apps for everything, and if you're not using them, you're missing out on the easiest way to keep your financial life in check.

### *WHY AUTOMATION IS YOUR SAVIOR:*

Set it and forget it: Use apps like Mint, You Need a Budget (YNAB), or even your bank's app to automate bill payments, transfers to savings, and everything else. Once it's set up, you can spend less time stressing and more time binge-watching Netflix.

◊ **Never forget a bill again:** Raise your hand if you've ever been hit with a late fee because you forgot about a bill. (Yep, me too.) Automation helps you dodge those fees because it pays your bills on time, every time. Your future self is already thanking you.

◊ **Savings on autopilot:** One of the best hacks? Pay yourself first by setting up automatic transfers to your savings account. That way, you're not tempted to blow all your money on impulse buys (looking at you, $30 sushi dinners). This is how you start stacking cash without even realizing it.

**Uncle Aaron's Hot** Take: "If you're not automating at least 50% of your financial life by the end of this chapter, I might have to come over and give you the talk personally."

## THE 50/30/20 RULE: BUDGETING'S GOLDEN TICKET

Still with me? Great. Now let's talk about how to divide your money. I know, I know—no one likes doing math. But trust me, this is easy and it works like a charm. Say hello to the 50/30/20 rule:

◊ **50% of your income goes to needs:** rent, groceries, utilities, gas, insurance—all the stuff that keeps you alive and functioning in society.

◊ **30% is for wants:** Netflix, dining out, travel, shopping. You've gotta live a little, after all. This is your fun money, the stuff that makes life enjoyable.

◊ **20% goes to savings and debt repayment:** This is the money you use to pay off student loans, build up that emergency fund, and invest in your future.

This breakdown gives you balance. It helps you handle the essentials while leaving room for some fun and a little financial security. Don't worry, this rule isn't set in stone—you can adjust the percentages depending on your personal goals—but it's a solid starting point.

My $20 Savings Revelation: Let me tell you something—when I first started budgeting, I was terrible at it. I'd blow through my cash by week three and end up borrowing from next month's paycheck.

One day, a friend of mine said, "**Why don't you just save $20 from every paycheck?**" At first, I thought, "**$20? That's nothing.**" But I tried it, and you know what? After a few months, I had a decent chunk of savings.

Turns out, even small amounts make a big difference when you stick to them. So if you think saving a little bit doesn't matter, I'm here to tell you: it does. Start small, be consistent, and one day, you'll be the person who always has extra cash stashed away for emergencies.

## WHY LIVING ON "VIBES" ISN'T A BUDGETING STRATEGY

I know what you're thinking: "But Uncle Aaron, I don't want to be a penny-pinching killjoy." And I hear you. But here's the deal: living on vibes—*a.k.a. winging* it financially—is the quickest way to blow through your cash. One minute you're buying concert tickets, and the next you're wondering how you're going to pay rent.

**Don't live on vibes. Live on a budget.**

"Living on vibes is fun until the vibe is 'broke.' Trust me, it's a bad look."

## FINANCIAL PLANNING:
*How to Budget for Your Life Goals*

Here's where we start connecting the dots between your day-to-day budgeting and your long-term goals. Think about the big stuff—buying a car, saving for a house, sending your kids to college (don't worry, they're still imaginary), and retirement. Your budget today is what gets you there.

### *Step-by-Step Guide to Setting Up a Budget*

Here's where we break it down, step-by-step, to help you get started on your very own budget. Whether you're just trying to keep track of your morning lattes or save up for a new car, this guide will make sure your budget is on point:

## 1. Calculate Your Income

Start by figuring out exactly how much money you're bringing home each month. This includes your paycheck, side hustles, or any other income streams. Be sure to use your take-home pay (after taxes).

## 2. Track Your Expenses

Write down every single thing you spend money on over the course of a month. Include both fixed expenses (rent, car payments, insurance) and variable expenses (groceries, entertainment, dining out). You can use an app like Mint or YNAB to help track this, or go old-school and keep a notebook.

## 3. Categorize Your Spending

**Break your expenses into three categories:**

◊ **Needs:** Rent, utilities, groceries, transportation—anything essential to your daily living.

◊ **Wants:** Dining out, movies, Netflix, and those impulse purchases that make life more fun.

◊ **Savings & Debt Repayment:** This is the money you set aside for savings (emergency fund, big purchases) and paying off loans or credit card debt.

## 4. Set Your Budget

**Now, apply the 50/30/20 rule:**

- 50% of your income should go to Needs.

- 30% can go to Wants.

- 20% should be for Savings & Debt Repayment.

If your spending doesn't fit this breakdown, make adjustments! If you're spending too much on dining out, cut back and move that extra cash toward savings.

## 5. Automate Savings and Bills

Make life easier on yourself. Set up automatic bill payments and automatic transfers to your savings account. This way, you won't have to think about it, and you're less likely to forget to save or pay a bill.

### *Uncle Aaron's Steps to Financial Planning:*

**Set your long-term goals:** Whether it's owning a house, having a family, or retiring on a beach somewhere, write down what you want. That's your "why." Trust me, you'll need it when you're tempted to blow through your savings on concert tickets.

**Create buckets for your savings:** This is where things get fun. You're not just saving for one thing—you're saving for multiple things.

**You need different buckets for:**

1. **Emergency fund** (aim for 3-6 months of living expenses)
2. **Retirement fund** (start early, even if it's small)
3. **Big goals:** House, car, vacation, future kids' education. It all counts.


**Reverse-engineer your goals:** Let's say you want to buy a car in two years and need $10,000 for the down payment. That's $5,000 a year, which means you need to save about $417 a month. Breaking it down into manageable steps makes it easier.

**EMERGENCY FUNDS:**
*Because Life Happens*

Life is unpredictable. Your car breaks down, you need dental work, or—God forbid—your phone falls into the toilet. Whatever the disaster, an emergency fund is your safety net. You don't need to save a fortune right away, but aim for $500 to start. From there, build up to 3-6 months of living expenses.

Start small, automate a little each month, and before you know it, you'll have a rainy-day fund that can handle more than a drizzle.

**BUDGETING WINS AND FAILS:**

### REAL TALK

Let's be honest—budgeting isn't always perfect. You'll mess up. You'll overspend. You'll forget to save. And that's okay. The key is learning from those moments.

**Budgeting Win:** A friend of mine used an app to track his spending and realized he was blowing $300 a month on takeout. He cut that in half, started meal-prepping, and put the extra cash toward a vacation. Boom! Extra $150 for travel.

**Budgeting Fail:** Once, I got so aggressive with my budget that I gave myself zero fun money. After two months, I snapped and spent way too much in one weekend just to feel "alive" again. Lesson learned  You've got to build in fun money, or you'll end up binge-spending when the pressure of being too strict gets to you. Balance, my friends, balance.

At the end of the day, budgeting is about control. It's about telling your money where to go, instead of sitting there at the end of the month, scratching your head and wondering where it went. Start with the basics—track your spending, automate what you can, and set realistic goals for both the short term and the long haul. And most importantly, give yourself some grace. No one nails this perfectly, and that's okay. It's not about being perfect; it's about making progress.

## FINANCIAL PLANNING AND BUDGETING FOR LIFE GOALS

Let's get real for a second. Budgeting isn't just about paying bills and saving for that next night out. It's about aligning your money with your life goals. Whether it's buying a home, getting a new car, planning for retirement, or even starting a family, your budget today is what's going to get you there. You can't just think in terms of "what's my paycheck doing for me this month?"—you've got to think long-term.

### *Budgeting for Life's Big Milestones*

**Buying a Car:** Let's say you're eyeing a new car in the next two years. Cars don't come cheap, and let's be real—financing might look tempting, but that down payment is still going to hit you like a ton of bricks if you're not ready. The average car costs around $35,000 these days. Want to put down 20%? That's $7,000. Time to start saving.

Reverse-engineer that goal. You've got two years, so that means you need to save around $292 a month. Automate it into a "car savings" bucket and let it grow. Before you know it, you'll be cruising in that dream ride.

**Saving for a House:** Let's talk real estate. If home ownership is on your radar, you're looking at big money moves. The down payment is just the start—don't forget about closing costs, inspections, and moving expenses. The key? Start early. Even if buying a house feels a few years away, building up that down payment now is going to make your life so much easier later.

Set a realistic goal for how much house you want and figure out the down payment. If a house in your area costs around $300,000, and you need 10% down, that's $30,000. Break it down into how much you can save per month and start automating that into a separate account.

**Retirement Planning:** I know, I know—retirement seems forever away, right? But here's the thing: the earlier you start saving, the more time compound interest has to work its magic. Even if you can only put away a small percentage of your income now, it's going to grow into something meaningful by the time you're ready to hit that golden beach with a margarita in hand.

If your job offers a 401(k) match, take full advantage. That's free money just sitting there. And if you don't have access to one, open an IRA and start contributing, even if it's just a little bit.

**Saving for Kids' Education:** Kids aren't in the picture yet? That's cool, but if you're planning on having them one day, the earlier you start saving for their education, the less it'll hurt when the tuition bills roll in. Look into 529 plans, which allow you to save for your child's education tax-free.

You don't need to have kids right now to start putting money away for their future. Every little bit helps.

## MONTHLY AND YEARLY PLANNING
*Tying Your Budget to Your Goals*

Let's talk about how your monthly budget ties into these life goals. It's not enough to just think about what you're spending next month—you've got to connect your short-term spending with your long-term goals. That's where yearly planning comes in.

**Monthly Check-Ins:** Every month, take a look at where your money's going. Are you sticking to your budget? Did you save as much as you planned? Did anything unexpected pop up (and did your emergency fund cover it)?

**Yearly Review:** At least once a year, you've got to sit down and look at the big picture. Have you made progress on your long-term goals? Do you need to adjust your savings? Maybe you got a raise (congrats!) or maybe you've got new expenses that need to be worked into the plan. The point is, budgeting isn't a "set it and forget it" deal—you've got to review and adjust as you go.

Look, budgeting isn't just about saying "no" to the things you want—it's about saying "yes" to the things that really matter. Want to retire early? Want to own a home? Want to take that dream vacation or send your future kids to college? It all starts here. Every dollar you budget today is a step toward building the life you want tomorrow.

Build yourself a "fun fund"—a little stash of money specifically set aside for treating yourself. It's guilt-free because you've planned for it. When it's gone, it's gone, but at least you won't be dipping into your emergency savings for that weekend getaway or fancy dinner.

## BUDGETING WINS THE DAY

At the end of the day, budgeting is about being the boss of your money. You're telling your money where to go, instead of wondering where it went. Start simple, keep it automated, and don't be afraid to adjust when life happens. You've got this—so go forth, budget like a pro, and start taking control of your financial future.

And remember, even Uncle Aaron messed up a few times along the way. But the key is learning, adjusting, and keeping your eyes on the bigger picture.

### *BUILDING ON BUDGETING:*
*Financial Planning: Leading to Long-Term Success*

Now that we've covered the basics of saving—both for the fun stuff and the oh-no-my-car-broke-down moments—let's talk about how saving fits into the bigger picture. In the last chapter, we talked about budgeting and how important it is to have a plan for where your money goes each month. Now, the beauty of having that budget in place is that it gives you the structure you need to focus on saving effectively.

Saving isn't just something you do when you have a little extra cash lying around—it's a built-in part of your financial plan. Every month, you should be saving toward both short-term goals (like that trip you've been dreaming about) and long-term goals (like buying a house, having kids, or retirement).

### *FINANCIAL PLANNING:*
*Linking Saving to Your Life Goals*

**Here's the thing:** Saving is part of financial planning. Budgeting helps you manage what you're doing today, but saving is what sets you up for the future. Whether that's in 6 months, 6 years, or 30 years, your savings goals should line up with what you want in life. So how do you link your savings to your life goals?

**Here's how Uncle Aaron breaks it down:**

◊ **Emergency Fund First:** This is your financial cushion—the thing that'll keep you afloat when life throws those unexpected curveballs. Aim for 3-6 months of living expenses, but start small if you need to. It's the foundation of your financial security.

◊ **Short-Term Goals:** Think about the things you want to do within the next 1-5 years—maybe it's traveling, moving into your first apartment, or buying a new car. These are goals that need focus, but they're close enough that you can work toward them relatively quickly.

◊ **Long-Term Goals:** Here's where the big stuff comes in—buying a home, planning for kids (and their education), or setting up your retirement fund. These goals take time and a bigger financial commitment, but the sooner you start, the easier they'll be to reach. Even if it's just saving a little bit each month, that's money your future-self will thank you for.

## UNCLE AARON'S GUIDE TO SETTING UP YOUR SAVINGS BUCKETS

To make saving easier (and more effective), I'm a big fan of setting up different "buckets" for different goals. This way, you know exactly what you're saving for and you won't be tempted to dip into one goal's fund for something else.

**Here's how you can organize it:**

◊ **Emergency Fund Bucket:** This is untouchable unless it's truly an emergency. We're talking job loss, medical bills, or major car repairs. You know, the stuff that you never see coming but always seem to happen.

◊ **Fun Fund Bucket:** Want to go on vacation next year? Have your eye on something fun, like a new gadget or concert tickets? This is where you save guilt-free for the stuff that makes life enjoyable. You'll enjoy it even more knowing it's not putting you into debt.

◊ **Big Life Goals Bucket:** This is for the serious stuff—down payment for a house, saving for your kids' college fund, or building up a fat retirement account so you can sit on a beach somewhere and sip margaritas. Whatever your big, long-term dreams are, this is where you put the savings that'll get you there.

***UNCLE AARON'S PRO TIP:***
*Automate Your Buckets*

**Once you've set u**p your savings buckets, automate the transfers. That way, every month, a little bit of your paycheck goes directly into each bucket without you having to think about it. It's like your money is working for you, quietly doing its thing in the background while you go about living your life. When those big expenses (or fun opportunities) come around, you'll already be ready.

## RETIREMENT:
*It's Closer Than You Think*

I know retirement seems like a million years away—but here's the reality: the earlier you start saving for it, the better off you'll be. Compound interest is your best friend when it comes to building a retirement fund. Even if you're only putting away a small percentage of your income now, it'll grow and grow over the years.

If your job offers a 401(k) match, take it. That's literally free money your employer is handing you to save for the future. If you don't have access to a 401(k), open up an IRA and start contributing. It's never too early to think about the day when you can stop working and start enjoying.

## UNCLE AARON'S FINAL THOUGHTS ON SAVING

Look, I know saving can feel like a grind sometimes—especially when all you want to do is enjoy the present. But here's the truth: saving gives you freedom. Freedom to handle emergencies without panic, freedom to do the things you love, and freedom to live your life on your terms. It's not about depriving yourself—it's about creating options for future-you. So whether you're saving $10 a week or $1,000 a month, every little bit counts.

**And remember:** saving is a habit. The more you do it, the easier it gets. One day, you'll look at that savings account and realize you're no longer just getting by—you're thriving.

Now go forth, my friends, and save like the bosses I know you are. Because future-you? They're counting on you to make the right moves today.

## WHAT WE COVERED:

We tackled budgeting head-on. From using the 50/30/20 rule to automating your savings, we made sure that your paycheck is no longer a mystery that disappears by the end of the month.

## WHAT I WANT YOU TO REMEMBER:

*Budgeting is your financial GPS—it shows you where your money should go so you don't have to wonder where it went. Get those spending categories in check and automate what you can.*

**Uncle Aaron's Action Plan:**

◊ **Create a Budget:**
Use the 50/30/20 rule—50% for needs, 30% for wants, and 20% for savings.

◊ **Automate Your Savings:**
Set up an automatic transfer to your savings account.

◊ **Download a Budgeting App:**
Whether it's Mint or YNAB, pick one and get started.

# 4

## <u>Saving for the Fun and the Future</u>

Alright, so you've read through the last chapter, and now you're basically a budgeting ninja. You know where your money's going, you've got a plan, and you're on top of your finances like a pro. But here's the next step in leveling up your financial game: saving. Because, let's be real—budgeting is just the start. The real magic happens when you start stacking up those savings, and that's what we're diving into today.

Saving isn't just for "boring adults" with mortgages and retirement plans. Saving is for you—whether you're stashing cash for that epic summer trip, planning for your first apartment, or building a cushion for when life throws you one of those "surprise" expenses. And trust me, it will. Think of saving as your secret weapon, the thing that makes sure you're ready for whatever life tosses your way—whether it's fun, planned, or an emergency that knocks you sideways.

**THE PSYCHOLOGY OF SAVING:**
*It's More Fun Than You Think*

**Let's get real for a minute:** saving money isn't always going to feel like the most exciting thing in the world. I get it—it can feel like waiting for Christmas, except the "presents" are a few months (or years) away. But here's the cool part: once you start seeing that money pile up, it becomes weirdly addictive. You'll feel like a genius every time you add another $50 or $100 to your savings. Watching your account balance grow? It's like leveling up in life.

**Pro Tip from Uncle** Aaron: Make saving feel like a game. Challenge yourself to stash away an extra $5 or $10 every week, just to see how fast it adds up. Every time you resist the urge to blow your money on something you don't really need, give yourself a mental high-five. It's like earning XP in a video game—but with real-life rewards.

## THE BENEFITS OF SAVING:
*From Rainy Days to Dream Vacations*

So, now that you've mastered budgeting and learned to control the flow of your money, the natural next step is to save. Budgeting gets you organized, but saving gets you ready—for anything. Emergencies, big purchases, future goals. Saving gives you the freedom to do the things you want, and more importantly, it protects you when life throws a curveball.

The best part? Saving isn't just about putting money aside for a rainy day—it's about giving yourself the freedom to live your best life on your terms. Whether that means upgrading your car, planning a dream vacation, or just knowing you've got the cash to handle whatever life throws at you next.

## EMERGENCY FUNDS:
*Your Financial Life Raft*

Let's get real for a second. Picture this: you're cruising along, life is good, and then boom—your car breaks down, your phone decides to take a swim in the toilet, or you suddenly need to go to the dentist because, well, life. Emergencies happen, and they're almost always at the worst possible time.

This is why you need an emergency fund. It's your financial life raft, ready to keep you afloat when life hits you with one of those "oh crap" moments. The classic advice says to have 3-6 months of living expenses saved up in your emergency fund, but let's be real: if you're starting out, even just having $500 or $1,000 stashed away can make a world of difference. It's the cushion that stops a minor crisis from turning into a major disaster.

## HOW TO BUILD AN EMERGENCY FUND
*(Without Crying)*

I can already hear you asking, "Aaron, how am I supposed to save that much? I can barely afford my avocado toast habit!" I hear you, I do. But here's the trick: start small. You don't need to have it all figured out today. Even saving $10 or $20 a week will add up faster than you think. Here's how to build your emergency fund without feeling like you're giving up all your fun:

**Automate it:** Set up an automatic transfer to your savings account every payday. Trust me, this is a game-changer. When you don't even see the money in your checking account, you won't miss it.

**Cut back on small things:** Skip one takeout meal a week or make your coffee at home instead of hitting up Starbucks. Those little savings can add up without making you feel like you're sacrificing.

## UNCLE AARON'S REAL-LIFE EXAMPLE:

When I was fresh out of the Marines, starting to raise a family, I learned the hard way that emergencies don't wait for you to be "ready." One month, we had car troubles, a surprise medical bill, and to top it off, my daughter decided to redecorate the couch with a Sharpie. The emergency fund? That was our saving grace—literally. Without it, we'd have been scrambling, stressed out, and probably going into debt. Instead, we handled it and moved on.

**Pro Tip: Got a ta**x refund or an unexpected bonus? Stash part (or all) of it in your emergency fund. It's like giving your future self a high-five for being prepared.

## GOALS AND RAINY DAY FUNDS:
*Saving for the Fun Stuff*

Now, let's talk about saving for the fun stuff—because saving doesn't have to be all about emergencies and the "what ifs." Maybe you're dreaming of that big vacation, or you've got your eye on a new gaming console, or maybe you're planning a weekend getaway with friends. Whatever your goals, you need a strategy to save for them without derailing your day-to-day finances.

Here's where rainy day funds come in. This is your stash for those smaller, non-emergency expenses. It's like your guilt-free spending account for the future, whether that's six months from now or next year.

## THE POWER OF GOAL-BASED SAVING

Saving is a lot easier when you know what you're saving for. Get specific about your goals. How much is that trip to Hawaii really going to cost? What's your budget for upgrading your car in the next year? Knowing the exact amount gives you something concrete to work toward, and it makes saving feel less like a sacrifice and more like you're working toward something you actually care about.

Divide your savings into different "buckets." Have one for

emergencies, one for fun, and one for long-term goals. This way, you're not tempted to dip into your emergency fund when that concert you've been dying to see rolls into town.

## CHRISTMAS SAVINGS TECHNIQUE

Let's talk about the holidays—because we've all been there. December rolls around, and suddenly, you're scrambling to buy gifts for everyone, and your budget is gasping for air. It doesn't have to be like that.

**Here's my foolproof holiday savings hack:** *Start in January.* No, seriously. I'm not saying you need to channel Santa Claus all year long, but setting aside a small amount each month for holiday expenses will save you a ton of stress when the season rolls around.

**Even $25 or $50 a month adds up.** By the time November hits, you'll be sitting pretty with a holiday fund that can handle gifts, food, and maybe even a little something extra for yourself (because, let's be real, you've earned it).

## 30-DAY SAVINGS CHALLENGE

Saving is tough sometimes—I get it. But sometimes all you need is a little push. That's where Uncle Aaron's 30-Day Savings Challenge comes in. We're going to turn saving into a game that's fun, easy, and effective.

**Here's how it works:**

**Days 1-7:** Set a daily savings goal—whether it's $1, $2, or even $5. The key is consistency. Every day, move that money into your savings account.

**Days 8-14:** Step it up. Increase your daily savings by 50%. If fun stuff and the oh-no-my-car-broke-down moments—let's talk about how saving fits into the bigger picture. In the last chapter, we talked about budgeting and how important it is to have a plan for where your money goes each month. Now, the beauty of having that budget in place is that it gives you the structure you need to focus on saving effectively.

Saving isn't just something you do when you have a little extra cash lying around—it's a built-in part of your financial plan. Every month, you should be saving toward both short-term goals (like that trip you've been dreaming about) and long-term goals (like buying a house, having kids, or retirement).

## FINANCIAL PLANNING:
*Linking Saving to Your Life Goals*

**Here's the thing:** saving is part of financial planning. Budgeting helps you manage what you're doing today, but saving is what sets you up for the future. Whether that's in 6 months, 6 years, or 30 years, your savings goals should line up with what you want in life. So how do you link your savings to your life goals? Here's how Uncle Aaron breaks it down:

**Emergency Fund First:** This is your financial cushion—the thing that'll keep you afloat when life throws those unexpected curveballs. Aim for 3-6 months of living expenses, but start small if you need to. It's the foundation of your financial security.

**Short-Term Goals:** Think about the things you want to do within the next 1-5 years—maybe it's traveling, moving into your first apartment, or buying a new car. These are goals that need focus, but they're close enough that you can work toward them relatively quickly.

**Long-Term Goals:** Here's where the big stuff comes in—buying a home, planning for kids (and their education), or setting up you were saving $2 a day, now make it $3. Keep this up for a week.

**Days 15-21:** Cut out one unnecessary expense for the week. Skip that coffee run, make lunch at home, or avoid that impulse Amazon purchase. Whatever you would have spent, move it into savings.

**Days 22-30:** Challenge yourself to save as much as possible. Use every trick in the book—round up your purchases, sell stuff you don't need, or pick up a side gig for a week. You'd be surprised how much you can rack up in just eight days.

At the end of the 30 days, you'll have a nice little stash that shows saving doesn't have to be a chore—it can be fun and satisfying. Plus, you'll be building a habit that will serve you for life.

## UNCLE AARON'S TAKEAWAY:

Saving isn't about depriving yourself—it's about giving yourself options. Options to handle emergencies, options to have fun, and options to live your best life without worrying about the next curveball life throws at you. Start small, build those habits, and remember: every dollar saved today is a dollar your future self doesn't have to stress about.

Now go forth and save like a boss! You've got this, and trust me, future-you is going to be forever grateful. Whether it's for that emergency fund that bails you out when life happens, or the dream vacation fund that lets you finally check something epic off your bucket list, saving money is all about creating the freedom to live the life you want—on your terms.

## BUILDING ON BUDGETING AND FINANCIAL PLANNING:
*Leading to Long-Term Success*

Now that we've covered the basics of saving—both for the

your retirement fund. These goals take time and a bigger financial commitment, but the sooner you start, the easier they'll be to reach. Even if it's just saving a little bit each month, that's money your future-self will thank you for.

## GUIDE TO SETTING UP YOUR SAVINGS BUCKETS

To make saving easier (and more effective), I'm a big fan of setting up different "buckets" for different goals. This way, you know exactly what you're saving for and you won't be tempted to dip into one goal's fund for something else.

### *HERE'S HOW YOU CAN ORGANIZE IT:*

◊ **Emergency Fund Bucket:** This is untouchable unless it's truly an emergency. We're talking job loss, medical bills, or major car repairs. You know, the stuff that you never see coming but always seem to happen.

◊ **Fun Fund Bucket:** Want to go on vacation next year? Have your eye on something fun, like a new gadget or concert tickets? This is where you save guilt-free for the stuff that makes life enjoyable. You'll enjoy it even more knowing it's not putting you into debt.

◊ **Big Life Goals Bucket:** This is for the serious stuff—down payment for a house, saving for your kids' college fund, or building up a fat retirement account so you can sit on a beach somewhere and sip margaritas. Whatever your big, long-term dreams are, this is where you put the savings that'll get you there.

**Automate Your Buckets:** Once you've set up your savings buckets, automate the transfers. That way, every month, a little bit of your paycheck goes directly into each bucket without you having to think about it. It's like your money is working for you, quietly doing its thing in the background while you go about living your life. When those big expenses (or fun opportunities) come around, you'll already be ready.

## RETIREMENT:
*It's Closer Than You Think*

I know retirement seems like a million years away—but here's the reality: the earlier you start saving for it, the better off you'll be. Compound interest is your best friend when it comes to building a retirement fund. Even if you're only putting away a small percentage of your income now, it'll grow and grow over the years.

**Uncle Aaron's Ret**irement Rule: If your job offers a 401(k) match, take it. That's literally free money your employer is handing you to save for the future. If you don't have access to a 401(k), open up an IRA and start contributing. It's never too early to think about the day when you can stop working and start enjoying.

## FINAL THOUGHTS ON SAVING

Look, I know saving can feel like a grind sometimes—especially when all you want to do is enjoy the present. But here's the truth: saving gives you freedom. Freedom to handle emergencies without panic, freedom to do the things you love, and freedom to live your life on your terms. It's not about depriving yourself—it's about creating options for future-you. So whether you're saving $10 a week or $1,000 a month, every little bit counts.

**And remember:** saving is a habit. The more you do it, the easier it gets. One day, you'll look at that savings account and realize you're no longer just getting by—you're thriving.

Now go forth, my friends, and save like the bosses I know you are. Because future-you? They're counting on you to make the right moves today.

## WHAT WE COVERED:

We covered emergency funds, rainy day savings, and how to make saving fun. We also talked about teaching kids to save using the jar method and how saving for fun stuff keeps you motivated.

### *WHAT I WANT YOU TO REMEMBER:*

Saving isn't about depriving yourself—it's about freedom. A little sacrifice today gives you more choices tomorrow. Build your emergency fund, set aside money for fun, and teach the little ones good habits early.

## UNCLE AARON'S ACTION PLAN:

- ◊ **Start Your Emergency Fund:** Even if it's just $10 this week, get started.

- ◊ **Create a Rainy Day Fund:** Set up a separate account for fun savings like vacations.

- ◊ **Teach the Jar Method to Kids:** Start with spend, save, and give jars.

# PART 2:

## BUILDING WEALTH
## &
## CREATING MULTIPLE INCOME STREAMS

Alright, folks, you've got your budgeting game down and you're saving like a pro. High fives all around! But now, it's time to kick things up a notch. Let's talk about making more money—the fun part. You've probably heard people toss around phrases like "side hustles," "multiple streams of income," and all that fancy financial jargon, but what does that actually mean for you?

Let me break it down for you, Uncle Aaron style: don't rely on just one paycheck. Whether you're pulling in part-time hours, working a weekend gig, or finally starting that business you've been daydreaming about, there's always a way to make more without selling your soul or working yourself into the ground.

### *BACK IN MY DAY...*

Look, back in the day, your job was your job. You clocked in, you clocked out, and if your paycheck covered the bills? Success! That was the goal. But these days? The game has changed, my friend. The internet and the gig economy have basically turned your phone into a money-making machine. Whether it's freelance writing, driving for Uber, selling your old clothes on Depop, or even monetizing a hobby you already love, there are a ton of ways to bring in extra dough without sticking to the old 9-to-5 grind.

But let's get real for a second—this isn't about chasing every shiny new opportunity that pops up. We're not here to burn ourselves out. Smart money moves are all about balance—making sure you're diversifying your income streams without spreading yourself so thin you forget what the sun looks like.

We're not trying to work 80 hours a week just to keep our heads above water. No, my friends, this is about creating flexibility and freedom. The goal? Work smarter, not harder.

# 5

## INCOME STREAMS AND SIDE HUSTLES

**THE SIDE HUSTLE LIFE:**
*Where to Start*

So, let's dive into the side hustle life. If you're not already part of this world, you're missing out. There's a side hustle for everyone—whether you're driving for Uber, selling custom art on Etsy, freelancing as a graphic designer, or even walking your neighbor's dogs. Trust me, there's a gig that fits your skills, your interests, and most importantly, your schedule.

**But here's the key:** your side hustle shouldn't feel like punishment. It should be something you're good at, something you enjoy, or at least something you don't hate. After all, you're giving up your time and energy for this, so why not do something that actually makes you feel good about the hustle? You don't want to end up resenting your side gig because it's sucking the joy out of your weekends. Believe me, I've been there, and it's not worth it.

*"That Time I Spent Three Years as a Wedding Photographer"* Alright, story time. I once thought I could make easy money as a wedding photographer. Sounds fun, right? I loved

snapping photos, and weddings seemed like the perfect gig—happy people, good vibes, what could go wrong?

Well, let me tell you, everything went wrong. I didn't count on Bridezilla demanding 1,200 perfectly edited shots or the fact that my weekends disappeared into a blur of endless "I do's," champagne toasts, and late-night editing marathons. And let me tell you, after a couple of 10-12 hour days lugging camera equipment and dealing with family drama, my body was not happy. My back was sore, my feet were on fire, and I was starting to question all my life choices.

Don't get me wrong—the money wasn't bad, but after three years of missing out on weekends and feeling more stressed than satisfied, I realized something: *while the hustle pays, it's gotta be worth the grind.* And, my friends, wedding photography was not worth losing my weekends and my sanity.

**Lesson learned:** If your side hustle leaves you more burned out than energized, it's time to rethink your approach. The hustle has to feel worth it, not like a prison sentence.

## HOW TO CHOOSE THE RIGHT SIDE HUSTLE

So how do you avoid making the same mistake I did? Choosing the right side hustle is key. You need to pick something that works for you—not just financially, but mentally and physically as well. Here's how to figure out the best fit:

### 1. What Are You Good At?

Start with your strengths. What are you naturally good at? Do you have skills that could translate into a side hustle? Maybe you're great at writing, design, coding, or even teaching. Whatever it is, lean into that. When your side hustle uses skills you already have, it doesn't feel like you're starting from scratch—and you're more likely to enjoy it.

## 2. What Do You Enjoy?

A side hustle shouldn't feel like punishment. If you're going to give up your evenings or weekends for this, you might as well enjoy what you're doing. Think about your hobbies or things you love doing in your free time. If you can find a way to monetize those passions, you've hit the jackpot.

## 3. What Fits Your Schedule?

Let's be real—you've already got a life. Maybe you've got a full-time job, family responsibilities, or other commitments. The last thing you want is a side hustle that eats up every spare minute of your time. Pick something that fits your schedule. Whether you can only hustle on weekends, after work, or even just a few hours here and there, there's a gig out there that'll work with your life—not against it.

## DECISION TREE FOR CHOOSING A SIDE HUSTLE

This tree helps readers decide on the best side hustle based on their time availability, skills, and interests. The branches guide them toward options like freelancing, tutoring, gig jobs, and more.

### TYPES OF SIDE HUSTLES TO CONSIDER

Now that you know how to find the right fit, let's talk about some popular side hustles you can start today. There are options for everyone—whether you want to work with your hands, use your brain, or just make some extra cash on your own schedule.

## 1. Freelancing

Freelancing is a huge space, and if you've got skills in writing, graphic design, web development, or anything creative, there's no shortage of gigs out there. Platforms like Upwork, Fiverr, and Freelancer are great places to find work, and once you build up a client base, you can set your own rates and choose the projects that interest you. The best part? You're your own boss. Freelancing gives you complete control over when and how much you work.

## 2. Gig Economy Jobs

The gig economy is alive and well, and if you're looking for something that offers flexibility, platforms like Uber, Lyft, DoorDash, and Instacart are great options. These gigs allow you to work on your own time, whether that's a few hours on the weekend or after your regular job. Plus, they don't require any special skills—just a car, a smartphone, and some hustle.

## 3. Selling Online

Got a knack for finding unique or vintage items? Love creating handmade goods? Selling online could be your new favorite side hustle. Platforms like Etsy, eBay, Poshmark, and Depop let you turn your creativity or thrifting skills into extra cash. Whether it's flipping items you find at yard sales or creating custom products, selling online gives you a chance to monetize your hobbies.

## 4. Tutoring and Teaching

If you've got a knack for explaining things, tutoring might be the perfect gig. You can tutor kids in your community, or even take it online with platforms like VIPKid or Chegg Tutors. Whether you're helping students with math, science, or even teaching English as a second language, this side hustle is rewarding—and it pays well.

## 5. Pet Sitting or Dog Walking

For all my fellow animal lovers, this one's for you. Apps like Rover or Wag! let you turn your love for animals into a side gig.

Whether it's walking dogs during the day or pet-sitting while their owners are on vacation, this hustle lets you spend time with furry friends while making extra cash. Plus, who doesn't want to get paid to hang out with adorable pets?

## UNCLE AARON'S SIDE HUSTLE CHECKLIST

Before you dive headfirst into your next side hustle, let me give you a little checklist to keep things real and sane:

Find something you enjoy: If you're going to spend your nights or weekends doing this, it better be something that doesn't feel like a chore.

1. **Keep your time in check:** You've still got a life to live. Don't overcommit and burn yourself out. Side hustles are about extra money, not losing your sanity.

2. **Make sure it's worth your time:** If you're spending hours on a side hustle and the pay is peanuts, it might not be worth it. Your time is valuable—make sure you're getting a solid return on it. Do the math before you commit to anything long-term. Trust me, nothing kills motivation like realizing you're making less than minimum wage.

3. **Keep it legal and organized:** It might sound boring, but trust me, the last thing you want is the IRS knocking on your door because you didn't track your side hustle income. Set up a separate bank account for your hustle, keep records of your earnings and expenses, and make sure you're setting aside enough for taxes. Yes, even side hustles get taxed, my friend.

4. **Don't forget about balance:** At the end of the day, a side hustle is there to boost your income, but it shouldn't take over your life. Keep that balance—make time for friends, family, and hobbies that don't involve money. Remember,

the goal is to work smarter, not harder.

## THE REAL GOAL: FINANCIAL FREEDOM

Here's the thing, though—side hustles aren't just about making some extra cash to cover the bills. They're about building financial freedom. And when I say financial freedom, I mean the ability to do what you want, when you want, without stressing over whether your paycheck can handle it. It's about having options, my friend. Side hustles give you the flexibility to take control of your financial future in a way that one single paycheck might never allow.

**Imagine this:** you're no longer relying on just your 9-to-5 job. Instead, you've got multiple streams of income. If your job ever goes south or if an emergency hits, you're not panicking because you've got other sources of cash flowing in. That's the real power of side hustles—they give you options, and in life, options equal freedom.

## FREELANCING VS. GIG ECONOMY COMPARISON

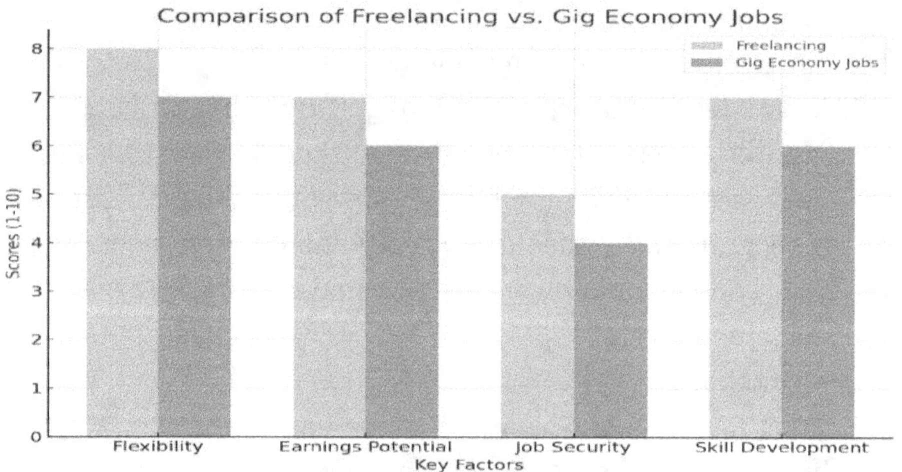


The bar chart compares the key factors of freelancing and gig economy jobs, such as flexibility, earnings potential, job security, and skill development. This provides a clear visual breakdown of the pros and cons

## SCALING YOUR SIDE HUSTLE

Now, let's get into something a little more exciting—what happens if your side hustle starts to grow? Maybe what started as a weekend gig has turned into something bigger. People are recommending you, your client base is growing, and you're starting to make some serious money. Congratulations!

At this point, you might start to wonder, "Could this be my full-time thing?" And the answer is: maybe. Some of the best businesses started out as side hustles. If your side hustle is bringing in consistent income and you're passionate about it, it might be time to think about scaling it into something more.

### 1. Consider the Commitment

First things first: turning your side hustle into a full-time gig is a big commitment. You'll need to take a hard look at your finances and make sure you're ready to make the leap. Do you have enough saved up to cover the slow months? Are you ready to hustle hard to make it sustainable? If the answer is yes, it might be time to go for it.

### 2. Invest in Yourself

If you're thinking about growing your side hustle, you might need to invest in yourself. Whether that means upgrading your equipment, taking a course to improve your skills, or even hiring someone to help with the workload, investing in your hustle is key to making it thrive. Just make sure you're putting your money into something that will give you a good return.

### 3. Build a Brand

Once your side hustle starts gaining traction, it's time to start thinking like a business owner. Build a brand around what you do. Whether that means creating a website, getting active on social media, or building a portfolio to showcase your work, it's all about creating an identity that sets you apart from the competition. Remember, people buy from people they trust, so building a strong personal brand is essential.

### 4. Set Your Rates and Know Your Worth

If you're scaling your side hustle, don't be afraid to raise your rates. As your experience and client base grow, your time becomes more valuable. Too many people undersell themselves because they're afraid of losing clients, but here's the thing: the right clients will pay for quality work. Don't sell yourself short.

### 5. Get the Right Tools

To grow your side hustle into something more sustainable, you'll need the right tools. This might mean investing in software to manage your finances, a system to keep track of clients and projects, or even an assistant to help you with the small stuff. The more organized you are, the more you'll be able to focus on growing the hustle instead of getting bogged down in the details.

## WHEN TO CALL IT QUITS

Not every side hustle is meant to last forever, and that's okay. Sometimes you'll realize that what you thought would be a great gig is actually more hassle than it's worth. And let me tell you, there's no shame in calling it quits if it's not working out. Your time and energy are too valuable to waste on something that's draining you.

Here are a few signs it might be time to move on from your side hustle:

◊ **You're consistently losing money:** If your expenses are higher than your income and you can't see a way to turn it around, it might be time to cut your losses.

◊ **It's affecting your mental or physical health:** If your side hustle is causing you more stress than it's worth, or if it's starting to wear you out physically, it's time to re-evaluate. No amount of money is worth burning yourself out.

◊ **You're not enjoying it anymore:** A side hustle is supposed to be something you're passionate about. If you're dreading every task and finding it hard to stay motivated, it's probably time to move on to something else.

◊ **It's taking over your life:** Balance is key. If your side hustle has started to take up every spare minute of your life, leaving no room for family, friends, or self-care, it's time to dial it back. Life is too short to be working all the time, even if it's for extra cash.

## UNCLE AARON'S FINAL THOUGHTS ON SIDE HUSTLES

At the end of the day, side hustles are an amazing way to increase your income and gain financial freedom. But remember: not all side hustles are created equal. You've got to find something that works for you, fits your lifestyle, and doesn't leave you completely drained.

**The key is balance.** Hustle hard, but don't hustle yourself into the ground. Build something that gives you the freedom to live life on your terms. That's what it's all about—options. Options to work when you want, take a break when you need it, and grow your financial future without losing your present.

Now go out there and make that money, my friends—but make sure you're having fun while you do it. That's the real hustle.

**WHAT WE COVERED:**

We dove into side hustles and why having multiple streams of income is a must. Whether it's freelance work, gig economy jobs, or starting your own business, there are ways to earn extra cash without losing your mind.

*WHAT I WANT YOU TO REMEMBER:*

Don't rely on just one paycheck. Diversify your income streams so if one dries up, you've got backup. Start with something small and manageable—before you know it, you'll have an extra cushion in your bank account.

**UNCLE AARON'S ACTION PLAN:**

◊ **Pick a Side Hustle:** What's something you enjoy or are good at? Turn that into extra cash.

◊ **Set a Side Hustle Goal:** Aim to earn an extra $100 this month.

◊ **Reinvest Your Side Hustle Earnings:** Put that extra cash toward your savings or an investment.

# 6

## Entrepreneurship: Turning Ideas into Action

Alright, future mogul, it's time to stop daydreaming about that genius business idea and start turning it into cold, hard cash. Now, let me set the record straight: we're not talking about some "get rich quick" scheme here (because those are as real as a 3-dollar bill).

What we're here to discuss is building something real—something that not only puts money in your pocket but gives you the freedom to live life on your terms. You might be thinking, "Entrepreneurship? That's for Silicon Valley tech geniuses, right?" Nope. It's for anyone with the guts and drive to try. And yes, that includes you.

**Here's the deal:** Entrepreneurship isn't just about having an idea. Ideas are everywhere—they're easy. What's tough is taking that idea and wrestling it into reality. It's not all sunshine, margaritas, and laptop-on-the-beach moments.

There will be late nights, early mornings, and days when you seriously question every life choice you've ever made. But, there's also nothing like the rush of taking something from zero to something.

Trust me, I've been down this road, and it's one heck of a ride.

## UNCLE AARON'S STORY:
*The Birth of Westchester-1.com*

Alright, let me take you back to 1996—yeah, I know, back in the *Stone Age* when WWW was still a mystery to most folks.

**"The internet? What's that?"** was the common reaction I got when I talked to people about my idea. To me, though, the internet wasn't just some fleeting novelty—it was going to be huge, and I saw its potential early on.

I had this idea to create a website for Westchester County, where new residents, people looking to move, and even local businesses could get all the information they needed in one spot.

That's how *Westchester-1.com* was born.

Now back then, building a website was like trying to speak a new language to most people. I'd talk to residents and business owners, and they'd look at me like I was trying to sell them moon dust. But I was inspired. I saw the internet as more than just a fad—it was the future, and I knew I had to jump on board.

The site started out simple. We had basic info: elected officials, schools, demographic details—stuff that new residents might find useful. But then, I had a lightbulb moment.

What if I started adding news? So, I started finding out press releases and adding them daily, that led to the next big idea: **interviewing local mayors.**

I'm talking **1997**, folks—nobody was doing this back then! There I was, with my *Hi-8 camera, a few mics, and a couple of* *lights*, running around Westchester County interviewing anyone who would sit down with me.

I was on a roll, feeling like a true entrepreneur. Eventually, the site grew, and I added business listings, giving local businesses a spot to promote themselves online. And wouldn't you know it—before I knew it, that little entrepreneurial venture led me into a corporate job that paid more than I ever thought possible. The best part? I landed that High Tech gig without a degree, just eight years after leaving the Marines.

**What's the point of the story?** Sometimes, following your gut and taking a chance on an idea can lead you to places you never imagined. My side hustle—*my entrepreneurial spirit*—opened doors I didn't even know existed.

## LESSON 1: SPARK IT UP
*Finding Your Winning Idea*

Every great business starts with a spark—that one idea that gnaws at you during boring meetings or while you're stuck in traffic. But here's the thing—you've got to make sure that spark is worth fanning into a full-blown fire before you pour everything into it.

**How do you do that?** *Test it.* Ask your friends, family, and anyone who will listen. If you're launching a product, get it into people's hands now.

Does it solve a problem? Does it make life easier, better, or more fun?

- ◊ **Solve a real problem:** The best business ideas fill a gap or solve a problem people are willing to pay for.

- ◊ **Test the waters:** Get feedback from real people. See if they'd buy your product or service before diving in.

◊ **Stay flexible:** Be prepared to pivot or refine your idea based on feedback.

*"The best ideas aren't just something you think is cool—they solve a real problem that other people are willing to pay to fix."*

## LESSON 2: THE SIDE HUSTLE STAGE

Listen, I'm not about to tell you to quit your job and go all-in on a business idea just because it sounds cool. *That's a quick path to being broke* and eating ramen for dinner every night. Instead, start your hustle on the side.

This is where you test the waters, work out the kinks, and make a little cash while keeping your main source of income.

◊ **Low-risk start:** Keep your full-time job while you experiment with your side hustle.

◊ **Build while you earn:** Use your regular paycheck to support your new venture without the financial strain.

◊ **Learn the ropes:** Experiment with your idea, refine your approach, and see what sticks.

Most big businesses started small. Take Shopify—it began as a snowboarding side hustle before evolving into the multi-billion-dollar empire it is today. Side hustles let you experiment, fail, and pivot without risking it all.

"Don't bet the farm on an untested idea. Start small, learn the ropes, and build from there."

## LESSON 3: ACTION IS THE KEY INGREDIENT

Everyone's got an idea. But what separates the people who talk about starting a business from those who do it is action. You'll never know if your idea will work until you roll up your sleeves and get dirty.

- ◊ **Take that first step.** Launch the website, start the social media page, make your first sale.

- ◊ **Take action:** Don't wait for the perfect moment or a flawless plan—just start.

- ◊ **Learn by doing:** Experience is the best teacher. You'll improve as you go.

- ◊ **Adjust on the fly:** Be willing to tweak your approach as you learn what works.

## UNCLE AARON'S STORY OF ACTION:

When I started my first photography business, I didn't wait for everything to be perfect. I had an old camera and a Craigslist ad. That was it. But guess what?

People started hiring me. Was my portfolio amazing? Nope. Did I figure it out along the way? You bet. Perfection is overrated—progress is what counts.

*"Dreamers talk. Hustlers do. Which one are you?"*

## LESSON 4:LOVING THE GRIND
*Entrepreneurship Isn't All Glitz and Glam*

Let me break it to you: being an entrepreneur is hard work. You'll see all these "gurus" on Instagram lounging by the pool with their laptops, but that's only half the story. The other half? Late nights, rejection, stress, and maybe a few breakdowns.

Success doesn't come to those who want it easy—it comes to those who show up every single day, ready to grind.

- ◊ **Embrace the hustle:** Success is built on consistent, hard work, not overnight miracles.

◊ **Be resilient:** Rejection and setbacks are part of the game—learn from them and keep going.

◊ **Stay the course:** Keep showing up, even when it's tough.

I once started a towing business, thinking it would be a cakewalk. *Spoiler:* **it wasn't.**

I was waking up at 4 a.m., towing cars in the middle of winter, and handling paperwork that could choke a horse. But through all that grind, I learned something: if you can keep pushing through the tough stuff, the rewards are waiting on the other side.

**"The grind isn't** pretty, but it's what separates the talkers from the walkers. You don't get to the top by accident—you get there by outworking everyone else."

## LESSON 5: BUILD YOUR NETWORK—IT'S WHO YOU KNOW
*(and Who Knows You)*

They say your network is your net worth, and I can't stress this enough. You can't do this alone. You need mentors, partners, and a community of like-minded hustlers who will help you when the chips are down. Get out there. Attend networking events, join entrepreneurial groups, and most importantly, don't be afraid to ask for help. Every successful businessperson had help along the way.

◊ **Connect with others:** Build relationships with people who can support, mentor, and guide you.

◊ **Ask for help:** Don't try to do everything alone—reach out to others for advice or resources.

◊ **Pay it forward:** Once you've built a network, help others too. It's a two-way street.

*"You don't have to know everything. You just have to know the right people who do."*

## LESSON 6: THE PIVOT
*When to Change Course Without Losing Your Head*

No business plan survives first contact with reality. Sometimes, you'll realize that your original idea isn't quite hitting the mark, and that's okay. The key to long-term success is being willing to pivot when necessary. Look at how Netflix pivoted from DVD rentals to streaming—and then to producing their own content. That's a billion-dollar pivot. Being flexible and adaptable in the face of challenges or new opportunities can be the difference between success and failure.

◊ **Be adaptable:** Don't be afraid to change direction when something isn't working.

◊ **Learn from failures:** A setback isn't the end—use it to inform your next move.

◊ **Recognize opportunities:** Sometimes the best opportunities come from unexpected places or in response to a challenge.

**I tried flipping** houses once. Thought it'd be easy money. Guess what? It wasn't. After a few tough deals, I pivoted to managing rental properties instead. I took what I learned, adjusted, and turned a losing venture into a winning one. Being flexible is crucial in business.

*"Success isn't about sticking to one path—it's about knowing when to change course without looking back."*

## LESSON 7: KEEP LEARNING
*You Don't Know It All (Yet)*

If there's one thing I've learned over the years, it's that you never stop learning in business. The minute you think you know everything is the minute you start falling behind. Read books, listen to podcasts, attend workshops—invest in yourself. The world of business is constantly evolving, and if you want to stay on top, you've got to evolve too.

## LESSON 8:ENTREPRENEURSHIP IS A MARATHON
*Not a Sprint*

Building a business isn't a one-and-done deal. It's a marathon, not a sprint. You're going to have setbacks. You're going to fail sometimes. But here's the good news: every single failure is a lesson that gets you one step closer to success. Don't give up after your first stumble. Get back up, learn from it, and keep moving forward.

- ◊ **Pace yourself:** Entrepreneurship takes time. Don't expect overnight success.

- ◊ **Stay consistent:** Keep working on your business even when progress feels slow.

- ◊ **Embrace failure:** Failures are inevitable, but they're also valuable learning experiences that help you grow.

## UNCLE AARON'S ENTREPRENEURIAL JOURNEY:

When I first started Westchester-1.com, it wasn't an immediate success. I had to work through countless challenges and setbacks. But I kept at it, learned from my mistakes, and slowly built something that became valuable—not just to me, but to my community. It didn't happen overnight, but the reward was worth the wait.

**"The real win is**n't in the money—it's in the freedom. The freedom to live life on your terms, call the shots, and build something you're proud of. But it only happens if you're willing to hustle, learn, and grind."

## ACTION PLAN:
*Turning Ideas Into Action*

To wrap up, here's a simple action plan you can follow to turn your entrepreneurial dreams into reality.

Follow these steps to get started on your business journey:

### 1. Identify Your Idea:

Think about your skills, interests, and what problems you can solve.

Test the idea by getting feedback from others.

### 2. Start Small:

◊ Begin as a side hustle while keeping your main job.

◊ Don't quit your day job until you've validated your business idea and gained some traction.

### 3. Take Action:

◊ Launch your business, no matter how imperfect it feels.

◊ Set small, achievable goals to build momentum.

### 4. Embrace the Grind:

◊ Prepare for long hours and hard work, but don't forget to enjoy the process.

◊ Push through the tough times—it's part of the journey.

### 5. Build Your Network:

◊ Connect with other entrepreneurs and potential mentors.

◊ Leverage the power of relationships to grow your business.

**6. Be Ready to Pivot:**

◊ Stay flexible and open to changing course if needed.

◊ Adapt your business strategy based on feedback and market trends.

**7. Keep Learning:**

◊ Invest in your personal development by reading, attending workshops, and seeking advice from others in your field.

◊ Never stop improving your skills and expanding your knowledge.

**8. Keep Going:**

◊ Remember that entrepreneurship is a marathon, not a sprint. Success takes time, but it's worth the effort.

**FINAL THOUGHTS ON ENTREPRENEURSHIP:**

**Look, I'm not going to sugarcoat it**—*entrepreneurship is tough.* It's not always glamorous, and there will be times when you want to throw in the towel. But if you're willing to put in the work, the rewards are worth it. Whether your business becomes the next big thing or just gives you a little extra freedom, the journey is one you'll never regret.

So, take that idea out of your head and start working on it. Test it, tweak it, and don't be afraid to fail forward. You never know—what starts as a side hustle might just become the next chapter of your life.

**Follow your gut.** Trust your instincts. And take that leap. You've got this, and Uncle Aaron's got your back the whole way.

**WHAT WE COVERED:**

We discussed entrepreneurship, from finding your winning idea to testing it out with a side hustle, and the importance of taking action. We also talked about loving the grind and when to pivot.

### *What I Want You to Remember:*

*Entrepreneurship isn't about overnight success. It's about grinding, learning, failing, and pivoting. Take action now, start small, and build something real. Trust me, the grind is worth it.*

**UNCLE AARON'S ACTION PLAN:**

◊ **Write Down Your Business Idea:** Start with an idea you're passionate about and solve a real problem.

◊ **Take One Action This Week:** Whether it's registering a domain or creating a business plan, get the ball rolling.

◊ **Network:** Reach out to someone in your field and ask for advice or feedback.

# 7

## INVESTING FOR THE FUTURE
### (AND WHY YOU SHOULD CARE NOW)

Alright, folks, gather 'round—let's talk investing. Now, before your eyes glaze over or you start scrolling through TikTok, hold on! This isn't one of those old-school, fall-asleep-while-standing-up speeches your dad or grandpa might have given about stocks and bonds.

Nope, I promise you, this is different. We're about to get into why investing matters to you—yes, you—whether you're still rocking your high school graduation cap, juggling three side gigs in your 20s, or just coming to the realization that stuffing $20 into a savings account every month probably won't cut it for that dream home with a pool and a golden retriever running in the yard.

We're going to shake up the way you think about money. Forget boring lectures, because investing isn't just for Wall Street types or people in fancy suits shouting about "market trends." It's for everyone, including you, sitting there in your sweatpants, sipping on yesterday's coffee.

Why? Because investing is about taking that little bit of money you've got and making it work harder than you ever will.

I'm talking about letting your money grow while you sleep, eat, or binge-watch an entire season of whatever show's trending. You don't have to be a financial wizard to start investing; you just need a little know-how and a willingness to play the long game.

*And guess what?* Uncle Aaron's here to help you figure it all out—without any of the boring, outdated stuff. So, buckle up, because we're about to dive into a world where your money finally stops being lazy!

## THE BASICS OF INVESTING:
*Start Small, Think Big*

**Let me tell you up-front:** investing is not a sprint, it's a marathon. And unlike running an actual marathon (something Uncle Aaron is too old for now, trust me), you don't need to train for years to get started. The earlier you begin, the better your chances are of reaching your financial goals without having to sell your soul to your day job.

**Investing Rule #1:** *"If you wait until you 'have enough' to start investing, you're already behind."*

**You don't need th**ousands of dollars to get started. Whether you've got $100 or $10,000, starting now is the key to reaping the benefits down the road.

## SOCIAL MEDIA'S INFLUENCE ON FINANCIAL DECISIONS:
*Don't Fall for the Hype*

I know, I know—you're constantly bombarded with videos of so-called "financial gurus" on Instagram and YouTube showing off their Lamborghinis, telling you how they "cracked the code" to making millions in six months. I'm here to tell you that most of that is pure BS. Anyone telling you they have a shortcut to getting rich is either lying, scamming, or has a trust fund they forgot to mention.

Look, it's tempting to believe the hype. But real investing is about patience, research, and smart decisions, not flashy promises. If a social media influencer is trying to sell you a financial course that promises you'll be a millionaire by next Tuesday, please do yourself a favor: scroll away, fast.

*"When it comes to financial advice on social media, trust but verify. And by verify, I mean double-check with a Licensed Financial Advisor."*

## AVOIDING THE "GET RICH QUICK" SCHEMES

Let me drop some hard truth here: there is no shortcut to building wealth. I don't care if it's crypto, NFTs, or some sketchy forex scheme—if it sounds too good to be true, it almost always is. Sure, you'll see a few success stories, but for every one of those, there are a thousand more people who lost their shirt trying to chase a quick buck.

Now, I'm not here to bash crypto or NFTs. They've got their place (which I'll explain), but understand that high risk comes with the potential for high reward—and high loss. If you're considering throwing your savings into the latest trending coin, remember that diversification is key. Don't put all your eggs in one basket, especially when that basket could disappear overnight.

## GETTING STARTED WITH INVESTING:
*The Tools You'll Need*

**Let's be real:** in the '90s, if you wanted to start investing, you had to call up a broker, maybe even dress up a bit, and prepare for a whole lot of paperwork. Today? You're literally a few taps away from becoming an investor. Apps like Robinhood, Acorns,

Stash, and Fidelity make it easier than ever to buy stocks, index funds, or even fractional shares with whatever pocket change you've got.

### *HERE'S A QUICK RUNDOWN OF WHAT YOU CAN INVEST IN:*

◊ **Stocks:** You're buying a small piece of a company. If that company does well, your stock goes up in value. If it doesn't, well, you get the idea.

◊ **Bonds:** Think of these as loans you're giving to a company or the government. They pay you interest, and generally, they're a safer bet than stocks.

◊ **Index Funds:** These are like the sampler platter of the investment world. When you buy into an index fund, you're investing in a bunch of different companies at once—spreading the risk.

◊ **High-Yield Savings Accounts (HYSAs):** These babies are a solid option if you want to grow your savings without the roller-coaster of the stock market. Think of it as a savings account on steroids—still safe, but with better returns.

◊ **Money Market Accounts:** Similar to HYSAs but with slight variations, such as how you can access your money or how interest is calculated. They're another stable place to stash your cash.

**Mantra:** *"Make your money work for you. If it's sitting in a regular checking account earning nada, you're letting the bank win."*

## UNDERSTANDING INDEX FUNDS:
*The Best Bang for Your Buck*

**Here's why I'm a fan of index funds:** they're simple, diverse, and perfect for long-term growth. If you don't have the time (or the inclination) to become a stock-picking genius, an index fund does the heavy lifting for you.

An index fund tracks the performance of a specific group of stocks, like the S&P 500 (which is a collection of the top 500 companies in the U.S.). By investing in an index fund, you're spreading your investment across a lot of companies. If one company takes a nosedive, you're protected by the others doing well.

**Let me give you an example to put this in perspective.** If you'd invested $1,000 in the S&P 500 back in 1990, by 2020, that money would've grown to over $10,000. That's the magic of compound interest and long-term investing. Now imagine you started investing $1,000 a year in an index fund starting at age 25—by the time you hit retirement age, you'd be sitting on a sweet nest egg without having to actively trade a single stock.

**Golden Rule:** *"An index fund is like a crockpot—it simmers slowly, but after years of letting it cook, you've got a rich, flavorful financial stew."*

## CRYPTO AND NFTS:
*What You Need to Know (But Not Do Immediately)*

**Let's address the elephants in the room:** crypto and NFTs. Are they legitimate? Sure, but here's the catch: they're volatile as hell. One day your crypto's worth a down payment on a house, the next it's worth lunch money. If you're going to invest in crypto, do it with money you're prepared to lose.

Same goes for NFTs (Non-Fungible Tokens, for those of you still scratching your head). They've had a huge buzz over the last couple of years, and yeah, some people have made serious bank. But be real with yourself—do you want to gamble your hard-earned cash on digital art? Because NFTs are still very much like the Wild West. There's potential, but there's also a good chance you'll lose your hat.

That said, educate yourself. If you want to dip a toe into the crypto or NFT world, that's fine—just don't jump in without doing your homework.

## THE MAGIC OF COMPOUND INTEREST

Let's break down why compound interest is your best friend. Think of it like this: when you invest, you earn returns on your initial investment, but you also earn returns on those returns. Over time, this snowball effect grows your money faster than you might think.

**Here's an example:** $1,000 invested today at 7% annual growth will be worth around $3,870 in 20 years. If you add $1,000 every year, you'll have $47,000 after 20 years. All that from just starting small and letting time do the heavy lifting!

## DIVERSIFYING YOUR PORTFOLIO:
*Don't Bet the Farm*

If I've said it once, I've said it a thousand times: diversify. The best way to minimize risk is to spread your money across different investment types—stocks, bonds, index funds, and maybe a little crypto if you're feeling spicy. This way, if one area tanks, the others will help balance things out.

Think of your investment portfolio like a meal. You don't just load your plate with fries (no matter how delicious they are). You need a balanced diet—a bit of meat, some veggies, and yeah, throw in a side of fries for fun. Same with your money.

**"Don't put all y**our financial eggs in one basket. And definitely don't put them in a basket that some influencer told you about in a 30-second video."

## TURNING SMALL WINS INTO BIG WINS:
*$50 a Month to a Golden Nest Egg*

**Let's get practical:** say you're putting away $50 a month into a 401(k) or an index fund with a 7% average return. You might think it's not much, but over 40 years, that $50/month turns into around $120,000. That's the magic of compounding.

And guess what? If you increase it to $100 a month, you'll end up with $240,000!

If your company offers a 401(k) match, that's even better—it's like free money. So don't leave that cash on the table!

## PHILANTHROPY:
*Giving Back as Part of Your Financial Plan*

Here's something most people don't think about when they're young—philanthropy. I know, you're probably still figuring out how to pay rent and make your next car payment, but listen: giving back should be part of your financial plan too. Even if it's just $10 a month to a charity that matters to you, starting small builds the habit of giving.

You might not feel like Warren Buffet today, but building generosity into your financial routine now means when you do hit it big, you're already in the mindset of helping others.

**"It's not about** the amount—it's about the practice. Start with what you can, and build from there."

## WORKING WITH A FINANCIAL ADVISOR:
*Why It's Worth Every Penny*

Now, I know some of you think you can handle this investing stuff solo, and hey, maybe you can. But here's the truth—working with a professional Financial Advisor is a game changer. Sure, you could spend hours trying to DIY your investments, but when you've got someone with expertise on your side, it saves you time, stress, and probably a few bad decisions.

A good FA (Financial Advisor) will help you navigate retirement accounts, make sense of market trends, and ensure your portfolio is balanced based on your goals. So, while it might seem like an extra expense up-front, think of it as an investment in your investment.

## FINAL THOUGHTS:
*Start Now, Thank Yourself Later*

Investing is like planting a tree. The sooner you do it, the sooner you'll be sitting under its shade. So, whether you're stashing $50 into a high-yield savings account or buying your first share of an index fund, just start. You'll be thanking yourself in 10, 20, or 30 years when you're kicking back, watching your money grow instead of stressing about how to make ends meet.

**And if you ever feel lost, remember this:** don't do it alone. Work with a Financial Advisor, get help from professionals, and be smart about your decisions. Uncle Aaron's rooting for you, every step of the way.

## WHAT WE COVERED:

We tackled investing—stocks, index funds, crypto, and everything in between. We also talked about avoiding get-rich-quick schemes and diversifying your investments.

### *WHAT I WANT YOU TO REMEMBER:*

Investing is like planting a tree. The sooner you start, the more time your money has to grow. Don't wait until you "have enough"—start small and let compound interest do the work.

## UNCLE AARON'S ACTION PLAN:

◊ **Invest $50:** Whether it's in a stock or index fund, get started today.

◊ **Automate Your Investments:** Set up automatic contributions to your investment account.

◊ **Diversify:** Spread your investments across different assets to minimize risk.

# PART 3:

## ADULTING ESSENTIALS

### *(INSURANCE, DEBT, AND LONG-TERM PLANNING)*

Alright, my friends, we've talked about making money, saving money, and investing money. But now it's time to talk about protecting your money. Because, trust me, life has a funny way of throwing curveballs right when you're least ready for them. And when that happens, insurance is what keeps your financial ship from sinking.

Whether you're 22 and just getting your first apartment or 32 and thinking about starting a family, the right insurance can mean the difference between a minor setback and a full-blown financial disaster.

**Insurance Rule #1:** *"If you've worked hard to build it, make sure it's protected."*

I know insurance can sound boring (and expensive), but think of it this way: insurance is like a safety net for your finances. You're paying a little now to save a lot later.

And trust me, paying a $20 premium for renters insurance is a lot easier than replacing all your stuff after a fire. Been there, done that.

This section is going to break down all the essential types of insurance you should be thinking about—health, car, life, renters, and more. Whether you're young, single, married, or planning for the future, insurance is one of those grown-up things you've got to get right. Because in the end, the best money move you can make is protecting what you've already worked so hard to earn.

**So let's get into** it—insurance, but explained the Uncle Aaron way, with stories, tips, and a few "don't make the same mistake I did" moments along the way.

# 8

## HEALTH AND CAR INSURANCE: WHAT YOU NEED TO KNOW

Alright, grab your coffee, tea, energy drink—whatever keeps you going—because we're about to dive into one of the least exciting, but most important, parts of adulting: health and car insurance. Yeah, I know, insurance talk sounds about as thrilling as watching paint dry, but stick with me here. This is one of those grown-up things you don't want to sleep on, because not having the right insurance is like driving a car without brakes—everything's fine until it's not, and suddenly you're in a world of hurt (and debt).

Don't worry, though—I'm not about to throw a bunch of boring jargon at you. I've got real-life stories that will make this whole thing way more relatable. Like the time I thought, *"Hey, I'm a great driver, I don't need car insurance,"* only to have reality (and a fender bender) hit me hard. Or that time I went with the cheapest health insurance plan because, *"What's the worst that could happen?"* and ended up with a hospital bill that could've paid for a brand-new car. Trust me, I've made the mistakes so you don't have to.

So, consider this chapter your friendly, no-nonsense guide to insurance, brought to you by your ol' pal, Uncle Aaron, with just enough cautionary tales to keep it interesting and (hopefully) help you avoid my past screw-ups.

## HEALTH INSURANCE: WHAT'S THE BIG DEAL?

Let's start with health insurance, because no matter how invincible you feel in your 20s, stuff happens. Whether it's a random trip to the ER or an unexpected diagnosis, health insurance is your financial shield. Sure, you're young and healthy (hopefully), but medical bills can wipe out your savings faster than you can say "deductible."

### *THE BASICS: HEALTH INSURANCE 101*

Health insurance works like this: you pay a monthly premium to the insurance company. In return, they help cover your medical expenses when you need it. You'll still pay some out-of-pocket costs, like deductibles, copays, and coinsurance, but insurance covers the big stuff—like surgeries, hospital stays, and all those doctor visits you'd rather avoid.

**Here's where Uncle Aaron drops some wisdom**: don't just pick the cheapest plan because you think you won't need it. That's like buying a super cheap umbrella in a storm—when you really need it, it's probably going to fail you.

### *KEY TERMS YOU SHOULD KNOW:*

◊ **Premium:** This is what you pay every month to keep your insurance active. Think of it as your ticket to the show— you pay it whether you use the insurance or not.

◊ **Deductible:** The amount you pay out-of-pocket before your insurance starts covering the big stuff. If your deductible is $1,500, that's what you'll pay for medical expenses before insurance kicks in.

◊ **Copay:** A flat fee you pay for things like doctor visits or prescriptions. You might pay $20 to see a doctor, while insurance covers the rest.

◊ **Coinsurance:** Once you hit your deductible, this is the percentage of medical bills you're responsible for. If your coinsurance is 20%, you'll pay 20% of the bill while insurance covers the other 80%.

### HEALTH INSURANCE OPTIONS

If you're in your 20s or early 30s, chances are you're navigating a few different health insurance options:

1. Employer-Sponsored Insurance: If you've got a 9-to-5 (or any full-time gig), this is probably where you'll find your health insurance. Employers often cover part of the premium, making this a solid option. Just don't forget to opt-in during open enrollment. And read those emails your HR department sends out!

2. Self-Employed or Freelancers: If you're hustling on your own or in the gig economy, you might not have an employer offering you a plan. But don't worry—the Health Insurance Marketplace (aka Obamacare) has options for you. You can compare plans, see if you qualify for subsidies, and choose one that fits your budget and needs.

3. Staying on Your Parents' Plan: Here's the good news—thanks to the ACA (Affordable Care Act), you can stay on your parents' health insurance until you're 26. If this option is on the table, use it! It'll buy you some time while you

figure out your own plan.

4. Medicaid: If your income is low, you may qualify for Medicaid, which offers free or low-cost health coverage. It's definitely worth looking into if you're starting out and not making much yet.

### HEALTH INSURANCE HORROR STORY:

**Picture this:** A friend of mine John was 27, healthy, and full of "I don't need health insurance" energy. Then, out of nowhere, he get hit with a nasty case of appendicitis. Guess who had to fork over $10,000 for an emergency appendectomy? Yep, that guy, (well his family did). Had he just paid for basic health insurance, he would've only been out a few hundred bucks.

**Lesson he learned:** *Don't mess around with health insurance.*

### NAVIGATING HEALTH INSURANCE AT WORK

For those of you lucky enough to have employer-sponsored health insurance, you've still got to navigate open enrollment, those benefits brochures, and make some big decisions. Do you want a high-deductible plan with an HSA? Or a PPO that lets you see any doctor you want?

### UNCLE AARON'S TAKE:

**If you're general**ly healthy and don't visit the doctor often, consider a high-deductible plan paired with a Health Savings Account (HSA). This allows you to save pre-tax dollars for medical expenses. But if you've got regular medical needs or prefer flexibility, a PPO plan might be worth the higher premiums.

## CAR INSURANCE:
*More Than Just a Legal Requirement*

Now let's shift gears (pun intended) and talk about car insurance. You need it—period. Whether you drive a 20-year-old beater or a brand-new Tesla, car insurance isn't optional. In fact, it's illegal to drive without it in most states. And trust me, skipping insurance to save money now will cost you WAY more later if something happens.

### THE BASICS OF CAR INSURANCE

Car insurance is all about protecting yourself, your vehicle, and other people in case of accidents. Here are the main types of coverage you'll deal with:

◊ **Liability Insurance:** Covers damage or injury to others if you're at fault in an accident. It's the bare minimum most states require.

◊ **Collision Coverage:** Pays for repairs to your car if you're in an accident, regardless of who's at fault.

◊ **Comprehensive Coverage:** Covers damage to your car from non-collision incidents, like theft, vandalism, or natural disasters.

◊ **Personal Injury Protection (PIP):** Helps pay for medical expenses, no matter who's at fault.

◊ **Uninsured/Underinsured Motorist Coverage:** Protects you if you're in an accident with someone who doesn't have enough insurance (or none at all).

### NO-FAULT VS. AT-FAULT STATES

**Here's where things get a little tricky:** some states operate under no-fault insurance rules, meaning your own insurance pays for your medical bills and lost wages after an accident, regardless of who caused it. This is common in states like Florida, Michigan, and New York.

If you're traveling or moving to one of these states, make sure you know what's required. Trust me, getting into a fender bender in a At-fault state and realizing you don't have the right coverage? **Not fun**.

### UNCLE AARON'S CAR INSURANCE QUOTE:

**"Driving without** insurance is like playing Mario Kart with a real car—you never know when a banana peel (or accident) is going to spin you out."

### WHY PERSONAL DAMAGE COVERAGE MATTERS

Here's the thing most people don't think about: Personal Damage Coverage (also called Personal Injury Protection) is just as important as covering your car.

It's not just about fixing the bumper—it's about making sure you don't end up paying for medical expenses out of pocket if you get injured in an accident. Medical bills add up fast, even from a small wreck. This coverage helps pay for things like hospital visits, lost wages, and rehab costs.

### UNCLE AARON'S CAR INSURANCE STORY:

**When I was 25, I** figured I'd cut costs by going with the bare minimum insurance. "I'm a careful driver," I told myself. Then one rainy night, I slid right into the back of a parked car (thanks, bald tires).

Guess what? I didn't have enough coverage for the damages and ended up paying thousands out of pocket. Moral of the story: Get good coverage, even if it costs a little more upfront. You'll thank yourself later.

### *WHAT YOU CAN EXPECT TO PAY (AND HOW TO SAVE)*

Insurance premiums depend on things like your age, location, driving record, and type of vehicle. If you're young, expect to pay a bit more since insurance companies see younger drivers as "higher risk" (thanks, statistics).

**But there are ways to save:**

- ◊ **Bundle Your Policies:** If you've got renters insurance or life insurance, bundle it with your car insurance for a discount.

- ◊ **Good Driver Discounts:** Keep a clean driving record, and your insurer might cut you a deal.

- ◊ **Good Student Discounts:** If you're still in school and rocking those A's, you could save some cash on your premium.

## UNCLE AARON'S TAKEAWAY:

Insurance might not be sexy, but it's a necessary part of adulting. Whether you're hitting the open road or just trying to avoid financial disaster from a broken leg, having the right coverage means you won't be left holding the bag when life takes a wrong turn. So, get insured, stay protected, and thank me later when you're not drowning in hospital or repair bills.

Let's move on to even bigger ways to protect your future—life insurance and family trusts. Spoiler: life insurance isn't just for your grandparents, and trusts aren't just for rich folks. Stick around for the next chapter—it's a good one!

## WHAT WE COVERED:

We dove into the world of health and car insurance—explaining the basics, key terms, and how to choose the right plans. We also discussed health insurance options for young adults, the differences between no-fault and at-fault states for car insurance, and why personal damage coverage is crucial.

### *WHAT I WANT YOU TO REMEMBER:*

*Insurance may not be exciting, but it's essential. Whether it's for your health or your car, having the right coverage can save you from financial disaster. Don't skimp on insurance— it's better to pay a little now than a lot later.*

## UNCLE AARON'S ACTION PLAN:

◊ **Review Your Health Insurance Plan:** Make sure you understand your premium, deductible, and copays. If you're healthy, consider a high-deductible plan with an HSA.

◊ **Check Your Car Insurance Coverage:** Ensure you have enough coverage, including collision and personal injury protection.

◊ **Compare Policies:** Use comparison tools to find the best deal without sacrificing coverage. Look for discounts like bundling or safe driver incentives.

# 9

## LIFE INSURANCE AND TRUSTS: SECURING YOUR FUTURE

Alright, buckle up, folks, because we're about to dive into some heavy but seriously important territory: life insurance and trusts. Now, I know what you're thinking—"Uncle Aaron, this sounds boring, and isn't life insurance just for old people?"

*Let me stop you right there.* Life insurance and trusts aren't just for seniors with one foot in the grave or billionaires sipping champagne on their yachts. They're for anyone who cares about protecting their loved ones and ensuring their family doesn't get left with a financial mess if something happens.

Here's a little gem of wisdom to start: The younger you are when you get life insurance, the cheaper it is. So if you're in your 20's or 30's and think this isn't for you, think again—this is exactly the time to pay attention. The cost of life insurance is practically a steal at your age, and locking it in now will save you big bucks down the road. Think of it as future-proofing your life, and who doesn't want to do that?

## LIFE INSURANCE ISN'T JUST FOR "OLD PEOPLE"

I know, I know—when you hear "life insurance," you probably think about your grandparents or those late-night commercials with sad violins. But here's the truth: life insurance is one of the smartest financial moves you can make, especially while you're young and healthy.

**Here's how it works:** life insurance is basically a contract between you and an insurance company. You pay a monthly premium, and in exchange, if you pass away, the insurance company pays a lump sum (called a death benefit) to your beneficiaries—usually your spouse, kids, or parents. The idea is to make sure that your loved ones aren't left scrambling to cover your funeral costs, debts, or other expenses if you're not around anymore.

## WHY GETTING LIFE INSURANCE EARLY IS A POWER MOVE

Here's the kicker: *the younger you are, the cheaper life insurance is.* That's right. Your age is your secret weapon when it comes to getting affordable coverage. If you wait until you're older or your health declines, your premiums will skyrocket.

Why? Because insurance companies see you as a bigger risk. So, getting life insurance in your 20s or 30s means locking in low premiums that won't break the bank.

**Uncle Aaron's Sto**ry: When I was 25, a few years fresh out of the Marines and starting a family, I thought, "*I don't need life insurance yet.*" Fast forward a few years, and my wife and I had two kids, a mortgage, and all the other financial responsibilities that come with adulting. I realized that if something happened to me, my family would be left holding the bag—rent, debts, and all.

I finally got life insurance in my 30's, and while it wasn't too late. The Premiums cost 30% more than if i had signed up in my 20's. I could've locked in even lower premiums if I'd done it sooner.

## THE TWO MAIN TYPES OF LIFE INSURANCE

There are a lot of life insurance products out there, but let's focus on the two most common types: term life and whole life. Both have their pros and cons, so it's about figuring out what works best for you.

### *TERM LIFE INSURANCE:*

◊ **What it is:** Term life insurance covers you for a specific period (usually 10, 20, or 30 years). If you pass away during that term, your beneficiaries get the death benefit. If you outlive the term, the policy expires, and that's that.

◊ **Why it's good:** It's cheap. Since it's temporary coverage, term life policies are usually way more affordable than whole life insurance. This makes it perfect for young people just starting out or those who want to cover specific financial responsibilities, like paying off a mortgage or raising kids.

◊ **Downside:** If you outlive the policy, you don't get any money back. It's like renting insurance, not owning it. Perfect for securing short term debt, mortgages, and business partnerships.

### *WHOLE LIFE INSURANCE:*

◊ **What it is:** Whole life insurance covers you for your entire life, as long as you keep paying the premiums. It also builds cash value, which you can borrow against or even use to cover premiums later on.

◊ **Why it's good:** Whole life insurance is more like an investment. Since it builds cash value over time, you're not just paying for coverage; you're building a little nest egg. Plus, the death benefit is guaranteed, no matter when you pass away.

◊ **Downside:** It's more expensive than term life insurance, so if you're just starting out or on a tight budget, this might not be the best option right away.

### *INDEXED UNIVERSAL LIFE INSURANCE (IUL)*

Before we move on, let me introduce you to a more flexible option—Indexed Universal Life Insurance (IUL). This policy is like the "cool cousin" of whole life insurance.

It gives you life insurance protection while letting you grow your cash value based on stock market performance (without actually being in the market). You can take advantage of market gains without the risk of losing cash during market downturns.

◊ **Pros:** Flexibility, potential for higher returns, tax-deferred growth.

◊ **Cons:** Can be more expensive and requires ongoing management.

**Uncle Aaron's Adv**ice: Here's the deal—if you're just getting started, term life insurance is probably the way to go.

It's affordable, and you can always switch to whole life or an IUL down the road when your financial situation improves. But whatever you do, don't put off getting life insurance. It's one of those things you don't want to leave until it's too late.

## TRUSTS

Now, let's talk about trusts. I know what you're picturing—trust funds are for people named Rockefeller, right? Well, here's a fun fact: John D. Rockefeller, one of the wealthiest people in history, set up some of the earliest, most famous trust plans that allowed his family to preserve their wealth for generations.

**But guess what?** Trusts aren't just for billionaires with private islands and yachts. They can be for regular folks like you and me. Trusts allow you to pass down wealth, protect your assets, and make sure your loved ones are taken care of when you're gone, without Uncle Sam swooping in and taking a huge chunk.

In fact, trusts are one of the smartest ways to build generational wealth. Think about it like this: you work hard all your life, you've built something—a home, some savings, maybe even a small business—and you want to make sure it ends up in the right hands when you're gone. A trust lets you do just that. You get to control how your assets are distributed and even set up guidelines for how your family can use the money. It's like leaving them a blueprint for success.

### *BUT IT'S NOT JUST ABOUT THE MONEY.*

It's about protecting your legacy. You might not have Rockefeller-level money right now, but that doesn't mean you don't have something worth protecting. A well-structured trust ensures that your hard-earned assets go exactly where you want them to, without going through probate (which, trust me, can be a long, messy, and expensive process).

So, let's break this down, Uncle Aaron-style. We're talking real talk, with some real-life examples, and maybe a dash of humor to keep you from tuning out.

Why? Because nothing says "I love you" quite like securing your family's financial future. This isn't just about what happens after you're gone—it's about making sure you've got your affairs in order and that your family is taken care of, no matter what life throws at you.

Still with me? Good. Let's get into how life insurance can be your family's financial safety net and how a trust can be the best gift you leave behind—even if your last name isn't Rockefeller.

### *SO, WHAT EXACTLY IS A TRUST?*

In simple terms, it's a legal arrangement where you, the grantor, transfer ownership of your assets to a trustee. The trustee is someone you trust—whether it's a family member, a friend, or even a professional—who will manage those assets according to your specific instructions. But here's the key: it's not just for you, it's for your beneficiaries—the people you want to benefit from what you've built.

**You get to lay down the rules:** maybe you want to set aside money for your kids' education, or you want to make sure they don't get access to their inheritance until they hit a responsible age (because let's be real, 18-year-old you might've blown it all on something ridiculous). Your trustee manages the assets according to your instructions, whether it's paying out income periodically or holding onto the funds until your beneficiaries hit a milestone, like graduating college or buying their first home.

### WHY SET UP A TRUST?

You're probably thinking, *"Uncle Aaron, I'm not rich. Why do I need a trust?"* But here's the thing—trusts aren't just for the ultra-wealthy.

They're a great tool for anyone who wants to protect their assets, minimize taxes, and make sure their money is distributed according to their wishes.

**Here are a few reasons you might want to set up a trust:**

◊ **Avoid Probate:** When you pass away, your estate goes

through probate—a legal process where the courts decide how to distribute your assets. Probate can be slow, expensive, and public. A trust lets your assets bypass probate, so they're distributed quickly and privately.

◊ **Control Over Your Assets:** A trust lets you set specific rules about how and when your beneficiaries get their inheritance. For example, if you don't want your kids blowing their inheritance on a new sports car the minute they turn 18, you can set up a trust that releases funds in stages.

◊ **Tax Benefits:** Certain types of trusts can help reduce estate taxes, which is a huge benefit if you have a sizable estate.

◊ **Protection from Creditors:** Assets in a trust are often protected from creditors, which means your beneficiaries won't lose their inheritance to debts.

## DIFFERENT TYPES OF TRUSTS

Just like life insurance, there are different types of trusts, and each has its own purpose:

### *REVOCABLE TRUST:*

Also known as a living trust, this allows you to retain control over the trust and its assets while you're alive. You can change or revoke the trust at any time. When you pass away, the trust becomes irrevocable, and your assets are distributed according to your instructions.

◊ **Why it's good:** It's flexible and helps you avoid probate.

◊ **Downside:** Since you retain control, it doesn't offer protection from creditors or taxes while you're alive.

### *IRREVOCABLE TRUST:*

Once you set up an irrevocable trust, you can't change it (without court approval, anyway). The assets in the trust are no longer considered yours, which means they're protected from creditors and estate taxes.

◊ **Why it's good:** Great for reducing estate taxes and protecting assets from creditors.

◊ **Downside:** You lose control of the assets.

### *TESTAMENTARY TRUST:*

This type of trust is created through your will and doesn't go into effect until you pass away. It's a good option if you want to control how your assets are distributed after you're gone but don't want to create a trust while you're alive.

◊ **Why it's good:** It's a way to control your assets after death.

◊ **Downside:** It goes through probate since it's part of your will.

## UNCLE AARON'S TRUST STORY

Now with my move into writing, I am protecting the assets gained from the proceeds. I set up a revocable trust to make sure my kids wouldn't have to deal with probate if anything happened to me.

It also gave me peace of mind knowing that the money I worked so hard for wouldn't be squandered in one go. My trust was simple: my kids get access to certain funds at 21, more at 25, and the rest at 30, ensuring they'd have some guidance before getting the whole kit and caboodle.

**Uncle Aaron's Wisdom:** Trusts are about control and protection. Even if you're not rolling in cash, they're a powerful tool for making sure your loved ones are taken care of. And the best part? You can still change your mind if life throws you a curveball—like it did for me, more than once.

## WRAPPING IT UP

Life insurance and trusts might sound boring, but they're crucial to securing your family's future. Whether it's making sure your loved ones don't struggle with debt after you're gone or protecting your assets from greedy creditors and probate court, these financial tools are essential.

**And here's the real kicker:** the sooner you set these up, the easier your future (and your family's future) will be. Don't wait until you're "old enough"—because if life has taught me anything, it's that the future sneaks up on you fast.

**So, take it from Uncle Aaron:** get life insurance while you're young, consider setting up a trust (even if you're not swimming in cash), and protect what you've worked hard to build. Your future self—and your family—will thank you for it.

# 10

## PROPERTY, RENTERS, OTHER ESSENTIAL INSURANCES

Alright, folks, it's time to dive into a topic that's about as thrilling as watching grass grow, but way more important: insurance. Yeah, I know—it sounds about as exciting as a root canal, but hang with me here, because this is the stuff that can save you from serious headaches down the line.

Whether you're moving into your first apartment, just bought a new car, or are debating whether that ATV you love should be insured (hint: it should), this chapter is here to break it down.

We'll help you see why insurance isn't just some "extra expense" but a crucial safety net for protecting what matters most. The right insurance can save your wallet, your sanity, and even your future when life decides to throw a curveball your way.

Skipping coverage might feel like you're saving money now, but trust me—when things go south, not having that safety net can hit harder than you expect. It's all about being prepared for those "what if" moments, and spoiler alert: they happen to everyone.

And don't worry, we'll keep things light and maybe even throw in a laugh or two, because life without the right insurance can go from fun to "oh-no-what-have-I-done" faster than you think. So buckle up—this is insurance, Uncle Aaron-style: practical, real, and way more necessary than you realize!

## INSURANCE MATTERS MORE THAN YOU THINK

Let me hit you with a little Uncle Aaron wisdom right off the bat: *insurance isn't about planning for the good days—it's about covering your butt on the bad ones.* When things go wrong—and trust me, they will—it's insurance that keeps you from losing your shirt. But here's the thing: insurance isn't just for homeowners or people with fancy cars. Even if you're renting an apartment or driving an older vehicle, you still need protection.

**Think of insurance as a shield.** You might not use it every day (heck, you might hope you never have to use it), but when that stray baseball goes through your window or someone backs into your car in the parking lot, you'll be glad it's there.

## RENTERS INSURANCE: YES, YOU NEED IT!

If you're renting an apartment and thinking, "I don't own the building, so why would I need insurance?"—here's your wake-up call. Renters insurance is a must. It's also super affordable, usually costing as little as $10-$20 a month. That's less than you spend on Netflix, and it could save you thousands if something goes wrong.

### *What Renters Insurance Covers*

Renters insurance typically covers three main things:

◊ **Personal Property:** If someone breaks into your apartment and swipes your laptop, TV, or that sweet gaming setup you've been working on, renters insurance has your back. It'll help you replace those items without dipping into your savings.

◊ **Liability:** This one's crucial. Let's say you throw a party, and one of your buddies trips over your dog's chew toy, breaking their wrist. Renters insurance will help cover their medical bills (so you don't have to).

◊ **Loss of Use:** If your place becomes unlivable due to something like a fire, renters insurance can cover your temporary housing costs. Imagine staying in a hotel for a few weeks—without insurance, that could drain your bank account real quick.

### *UNCLE AARON'S STORY:*
*The Time I Thought Renters Insurance Was a Scam*

**I'll admit it. Wh**en I first started renting back in the day, I thought renters insurance was a scam. "Why pay for something I'll probably never need?" I told myself.

Fast forward to the day a neighbor's washing machine flooded my apartment, and suddenly, my "scam" renters insurance saved me about $3,000 in damages. Lesson learned: it's better to have it and not need it than to need it and not have it.

### *WHY BUNDLING INSURANCE IS THE SMART MOVE*

I know , I covered it already... Its that important! I know what you're thinking: "Okay, I'm already paying for car insurance, and now you want me to shell out for renters insurance too?" But here's the good news—most insurance companies offer discounts when you bundle.

That means if you get both your car and renters insurance from the same company, you'll pay less than if you had them separately. Same goes for bundling car insurance with homeowners, ATV, or motorcycle insurance. It's like a financial two-for-one deal, and who doesn't love those?

## SPECIALTY INSURANCE:
*Should You Insure That ATV, Boat, or Side Hustle?*

So, you've got an ATV or a boat—or maybe you're running a little side hustle out of your garage. Should you insure those too?

**Short answer: Yes, you probably should.**

*ATV Insurance*

If you've got an ATV, dirt bike, or any other off-road vehicle, you're probably thinking, *"What's the worst that could happen? I'm just riding around the woods."*

**But here's the thing:** ATV accidents happen. Whether you hit a tree or flip it on a trail, the repair costs can add up fast. And if you damage someone else's property or get into an accident with another rider, you could be on the hook for their damages too.

**ATV insurance covers:**

◊ Liability for property damage and injuries to others.

◊ Damage to your ATV from accidents, theft, or weather.

◊ Medical payments for you and your passengers.

### BOAT INSURANCE

Got a boat? Boat insurance is a must, especially if you live near water. Whether it's a sailboat, motorboat, or even a jet ski, boat insurance covers damages, theft, and liability—because let's be honest, accidents happen on the water too.

### SIDE HUSTLE INSURANCE

If you're running a side hustle, especially if it involves clients or inventory, you might need business insurance. Things like general liability insurance or home-based business insurance can protect you if a customer gets hurt or you lose a shipment of products.

## UNCLE AARON'S TAKEAWAY:

*Insurance Isn't Sexy, but It's Essential*

Look, I get it—insurance is not the most exciting thing to talk about. But here's the reality: it's one of the most important financial decisions you'll ever make. Skimping on coverage because you think "it won't happen to me" is like walking a tightrope without a net. You might make it across just fine, but if you slip, you're in for a world of hurt.

And hey, here's one last Uncle Aaron quote for the road: "Insurance isn't about the 'what ifs'—it's about the 'when it happens.'" So, make sure you're covered, whether it's your car, your apartment, or that sweet ATV you can't wait to take for a spin. Your future self will thank you.

## WHAT WE COVERED:

We broke down why you need insurance—health, car, and life—and what happens if you don't have it. We also talked about how to find the right coverage without overpaying.

### *WHAT I WANT YOU TO REMEMBER:*

Insurance is your safety net. You don't need to go overboard, but having the right coverage keeps you from facing financial disaster when life throws you a curveball.

## UNCLE AARON'S ACTION PLAN:

◊ **Review Your Insurance Policies:** Make sure your health, car, and life insurance fit your current needs.

◊ **Shop Around for Better Rates:** Don't assume your current insurer is giving you the best deal.

◊ **Consider Life Insurance:** If you have dependents, look into a term life insurance policy.

# 11

## UNDERSTANDING DEBT AND HOW TO PAY IT OFF

Alright, here's where things get real. Debt. We've all heard horror stories about it, and let's be honest, debt can be a sneaky little monster. One minute you're swiping your credit card for a quick coffee, and the next, you're staring down the barrel of a $2,000 balance, wondering where it all went. Trust me, I've been there. But here's the good news: with a solid plan, you can slay that debt monster and keep it from running your life.

Debt is neither good nor bad on its own—it's how you manage it that makes the difference. There's good debt (think student loans or a mortgage) that's an investment in your future, and then there's bad debt (think maxed-out credit cards or high-interest personal loans) that can dig you into a deep financial hole.

This chapter is your crash course on understanding debt, how to pay it off, and how to avoid the pitfalls that can leave you feeling stuck. We'll dive into student loans, credit card debt, good vs. bad debt, and even some hacks to speed up your repayment.

## WHAT IS DEBT REALLY?

**Let's start with the basics.** Debt is essentially borrowed money that you agree to pay back over time, often with interest. There are two main categories: secured debt (like a mortgage, where the loan is backed by an asset like your house) and unsecured debt (like credit card debt, which isn't tied to any collateral). Knowing the type of debt you have helps you prioritize how to tackle it.

### *GOOD DEBT VS. BAD DEBT*

Not all debt is created equal. Good debt is the kind that helps you build wealth over time. For example:

◊ **Student loans:** While it's no fun paying these off, a degree can lead to better-paying jobs over your lifetime.

◊ **Mortgages:** Investing in property typically pays off in the long run, as homes often appreciate in value.

◊ **Business loans:** Borrowing to start or grow a business can increase your income and wealth if managed correctly.

Bad debt, on the other hand, includes high-interest debt that doesn't add long-term value to your life, like:

◊ Credit card debt: Especially when you're just making the minimum payments—more on that soon.

◊ Personal loans for unnecessary expenses or extravagant purchases.

**Uncle Aaron's Tip**: Ask yourself, "Is this debt helping me grow?" If it's not contributing to your future wealth or stability, think twice before taking it on.

## STUDENT LOANS:
*The Elephant in the Room*

**Let's face it:** student loans are one of the biggest financial burdens young people face today. But they're also one of the most misunderstood. Knowing the difference between federal and private loans, how interest accrues, and what repayment options are available can make all the difference.

### FEDERAL VS. PRIVATE LOANS

◊ **Federal loans:** These come with perks like lower interest rates, income-driven repayment plans, and potential for loan forgiveness. They're usually the best option if you need to borrow for school.

◊ **Private loans:** These are offered by banks or credit unions and often come with higher interest rates and fewer repayment options. Avoid these unless you've maxed out your federal options.

## LOAN REPAYMENT STRATEGIES

When it comes to paying off student loans, the goal is to minimize interest and pay off the principal as quickly as possible. Here's where strategy comes into play:

◊ **Standard Repayment Plan:** This is the default plan, where you'll pay off your loans in 10 years. It's the fastest route but may have higher monthly payments.

◊ **Income-Driven Repayment Plans:** If you're struggling with high monthly payments, these plans adjust your payments based on your income. Be aware, though—lower payments can mean paying more in interest over time.

◊ **Refinancing:** If you have private loans, refinancing them for a lower interest rate can save you a bundle. But be careful: refinancing federal loans will strip away their protections, like income-based repayment options and loan forgiveness.

### *DEBT SNOWBALL AND DEBT AVALANCHE*

Two of the most popular strategies to pay off debt are the Debt Snowball and Debt Avalanche methods. Both work, but here's the breakdown:

◊ **Debt Snowball:** You start by paying off your smallest debt first while making minimum payments on the rest. Once that small debt is gone, you roll that payment into your next biggest debt. The psychological wins from knocking out debts can keep you motivated.

◊ **Debt Avalanche:** This method focuses on paying off the debt with the highest interest rate first. While you might not see those quick wins, you'll save more money on interest over time.

**I used the Debt S**nowball method back when I was knee-deep in credit card bills. Seeing those smaller balances disappear kept me going when things got tough!

### *CREDIT CARD DEBT: YOUR WORST FRIENEMY*

Credit cards can be awesome—if used responsibly. They help build credit, offer rewards, and are handy in emergencies. But if you're not careful, they can also spiral into a debt trap.

### *MINIMUM PAYMENTS: THE SILENT KILLER*

Here's the thing about minimum payments: they're designed to keep you in debt. When you only pay the minimum, the bulk of your payment goes toward interest, not the principal (the actual amount you borrowed).

This means it'll take years to pay off even a modest balance.

Let's say you have $5,000 in credit card debt at 18% interest. If you only make the minimum payment each month, it could take you over 20 years to pay off the balance, and you'll end up paying thousands in interest alone.

### *Twice-a-Month Payments: A Simple Hack*

Here's a trick: instead of making one big payment each month, try making two smaller payments—one right after your statement closes and another two weeks later. This reduces the average daily balance on your card, meaning you'll pay less interest over time. It's like squeezing a little extra cash out of your monthly budget without even feeling the pinch.

**Always aim to pay** more than the minimum. And if you're using a card regularly, pay it off in full each month to avoid getting slammed by interest.

## BUILDING AND REPAIRING CREDIT

Your credit score is like your financial report card. It tells lenders how risky you are as a borrower. A good credit score means lower interest rates, better loan options, and even potential savings on insurance.

### *How to Build Credit*

◊ **Use Credit Responsibly:** This means paying off your balances on time and in full whenever possible. One missed payment can drop your score by 50 to 100 points.

◊ **Keep Balances Low:** Don't max out your credit cards. Try to use less than 30% of your available credit at any given time.

◊ **Diversify Your Credit:** Having different types of credit (credit-cards, car loans, student loans) can help improve your score—as long as you manage them well.

### *HOW TO REPAIR CREDIT*

If you've made some mistakes (hey, we've all been there), don't panic. You can repair your credit with a few simple steps:

◊ **Pay Down Debt:** Start with high-interest debt and work your way down.

◊ **Dispute Errors:** Sometimes, credit reports contain mistakes. Check your report regularly, and if you spot an error, dispute it.

◊ **Be Patient:** Credit repair takes time, but consistent effort pays off. Most negative marks fall off your report after seven years, and the impact of late payments diminishes over time.

### *STUDENT LOAN FORGIVENESS PROGRAMS (2024 UPDATE)*

The landscape for student loan forgiveness has been changing, especially in recent years. As of 2024, here are some key options:

◊ **Public Service Loan Forgiveness (PSLF):** If you work for the government or a non-profit and make 120 qualifying payments, the remainder of your loan balance can be forgiven.

◊ **Income-Driven Repayment Forgiveness:** After making payments for 20-25 years on an income-driven repayment plan, your remaining loan balance may be forgiven.

◊ **Biden Student Loan Forgiveness:** There are ongoing discussions about wider-scale loan forgiveness. As of early 2024, the details are still in flux, but there's potential for broader relief in the coming years. Keep an eye on these updates and talk to a financial planner or your loan servicer to see what options you qualify for.

**Uncle Aaron's Rem**inder: Stay informed! Programs and policies are changing all the time, and you don't want to miss out on opportunities to save money or wipe out debt faster.

### *PARENT PLUS LOANS AND HOW TO HANDLE THEM*

If your parents took out Parent PLUS Loans for your education, they're probably feeling the weight of that debt, too. These loans are federal loans, but they're solely in your parents' names—not yours. Here's how to help your folks deal with them:

◊ **Refinancing:** This can lower interest rates, but it also turns the federal loan into a private loan, which means losing some protections.

◊ **Income-Contingent Repayment:** Parents can switch to this plan, which adjusts payments based on their income, with forgiveness after 25 years.

## FINAL THOUGHTS: GET SMART ABOUT DEBT

Debt doesn't have to be a death sentence. With the right tools and strategies, you can take control of your debt and come out the other side stronger.

Whether you're managing student loans, juggling credit cards, or figuring out how to help your parents with their debt, the key is to stay informed and stay disciplined.

## UNCLE AARON'S FINAL WORD:

If I could go back and tell 20-year-old me one thing, it would be this: pay attention to your debt. The sooner you get a handle on it, the sooner you'll be free to live the life you want—without debt hanging over your head. Trust me, your future self will thank you.

# PART 4

## ACHIEVING FINANCIAL FREEDOM

Alright, buckle up! Let's get into one of the trickiest, most delicate topics when it comes to money: relationships. Whether it's your parents, partner, friends, or even that cousin who still owes you twenty bucks, money affects relationships in more ways than you'd think. It's not just about who pays for dinner or who gets stuck with the bill after a weekend trip—money can dig deep into trust, power dynamics, and long-term happiness.

**Here's the thing:** money is personal. How we spend, save, and manage it says a lot about who we are. And when you're in a relationship, your financial habits are constantly bumping up against someone else's. Trust me, I've seen it all—from the joys of splitting Christmas savings with my spouse to the not-so-joyful realities of child support after divorce. Good communication about money is non-negotiable if you want to keep things smooth and avoid the mess that money fights can create.

You might think money conversations are awkward or that it's easier to avoid them, but that's like ignoring a ticking time bomb and hoping it never goes off.

**Spoiler: it will.** Whether you're figuring out how to lend money to a friend without losing the friendship, splitting rent with your partner, or deciding how to invest your savings together, talking about money early and often can save you from headaches and heartaches later.

And don't worry, we'll keep it light—because, yes, money can be funny, especially when you're figuring it out with the people you love (or tolerate). But at the end of the day, good money communication is like the oil that keeps the relationship machine running smoothly.

You don't want to be stuck on the side of the road because you never bothered to check the financial engine, right? Let's dive into how to make sure your relationships—and your wallet—stay in good shape!

# 12

## NAVIGATING MONEY CONVERSATIONS: FRIENDS AND FAMILY

Alright, let's all have a seat on the couch... yes, put down your phones for a second. We're about to dive into one of those uncomfortable but oh-so-necessary conversations: talking about money with the people you love, like, or just have to deal with anyway.

Whether it's figuring out who's chipping in for the group vacation, negotiating rent with that roommate who "accidentally" forgets every month, or trying to explain to your parents that you're totally capable of managing your own money now (even though you just bought three takeout meals in a row)—these money talks are awkward, but let me tell you, they don't have to turn into a disaster.

Money conversations are like navigating through a room full of Legos—you've got to step carefully, or things can get painful real fast. But here's the kicker: if you tackle them head-on with a mix of honesty, clear expectations, and a little humor, you can get through without stepping on anyone's toes—or bank accounts.

Whether it's a chat with friends about splitting bills or talking to your significant other about budgeting, you can come out the other side stronger. Trust me, nothing strains friendships more than that one friend who "forgets" their part of the Airbnb payment after everyone's already Venmo'd you.

*And look, I get it.* These talks aren't easy. Sometimes they're flat-out awkward. Throw in a couple of side-eye glances and maybe an awkward pause or two, and you've got yourself the perfect recipe for discomfort.

But it's a necessary evil. Because the alternative—letting things slide until you're stuck with the entire restaurant bill or watching rent pile up while your roommate buys a new gaming system—is even worse.

So let's dive into these chats, tackle them head-on, and maybe even find a way to make it a little less painful (and maybe a little funny) along the way.

## MONEY AND FRIENDS:
*Keep It Light, But Keep It Honest*

First up, let's tackle your friend circle. There's no easier way to make things weird with your buddies than by lending or borrowing money. One minute you're splitting pizza, the next you're subtly avoiding eye contact because someone hasn't paid you back for last weekend's Uber. But hey, it doesn't have to be like that.

### *LENDING MONEY WITHOUT LOSING FRIENDS*

If a friend asks to borrow some cash, you need to ask yourself two important questions: Can you afford to lose that money? And do you value the friendship more than getting repaid? If the answer to either of those is "no," you've got your answer.

The truth is, money and friendships don't always mix, but if they do, set clear expectations up front. Be polite, but firm—because clarity is the secret sauce to keeping your relationship intact.

**Uncle Aaron's Rule of Lending:** *Never lend more than you can afford to never see again.*

## HOW TO NEGOTIATE WITHOUT FEELING WEIRD

Now let's talk about negotiation. Whether it's figuring out rent splits with your roommates or trying to land a salary bump at work, negotiation is a skill everyone should have in their back pocket. The key here is that negotiation isn't about being pushy; it's about finding common ground that works for everyone.

### *NEGOTIATING RENT WITH ROOMMATES*

Ever had that one roommate who somehow always seems to get the master bedroom while you're stuck with the tiny one next to the street? Rent negotiations are tricky but totally doable. Here's how to make it happen without causing tension:

◊ **Be upfront:** When you're moving in, lay everything on the table—how much you're each willing to pay, what space each person will get, and who's responsible for what bills.

◊ **Fair doesn't always mean equal:** If someone gets the bigger room, maybe they should pay a bit more. It's about splitting the load in a way that makes everyone feel good about what they're getting.

◊ **Put it in writing:** Trust me, you don't want to rely on vague memory when rent day comes around. Get the agreement down on paper.

## SALARY NEGOTIATIONS:
*Know Your Worth*

Now, salary negotiation—this is the big leagues, folks. It can feel like you're stepping into a boxing ring with your boss, but it doesn't have to be a showdown. You're negotiating for your future here, so it's time to shake off that nervous energy and walk in with confidence. Here's how to crush it:

◊ **Do your homework:** Know what people in your industry and area are getting paid for similar work. You're not guessing here—you're coming in with data.

◊ **Practice your pitch:** Go in with a plan. Be ready to explain why you deserve a raise and how you've added value to the company. Confidence is key, but so is preparation.

◊ **Be flexible:** Maybe they can't give you a raise right now, but they can offer extra vacation days, a flexible work schedule, or another perk. Negotiation is about finding the win-win.

## TALKING MONEY WITH FAMILY:
*When to Push and When to Let Go*

Family money conversations can feel like walking on eggshells, especially when you're talking to your parents about finances. Whether they're helping you out with college, or you're ready to set some financial boundaries, the goal is mutual respect.

### ASKING FOR HELP
*(Without Feeling Like a Mooch)*

Let's be real: asking for money from family is awkward. But sometimes you need a hand. Maybe you're in college, saving for a down payment on your first apartment, or tackling unexpected medical bills. The trick is to ask in a way that's respectful, clear, and doesn't make either of you uncomfortable:

◊ **Be honest about why you need the money:** Whether it's rent or an emergency fund, be transparent about where the money is going.

◊ **Set a payback plan:** Even if your parents say, "Don't worry about it," offer to repay them—either in full or in installments. This shows responsibility and builds trust.

**Uncle Aaron's Advice:** It's not about asking for help—it's about knowing when to ask. There's no shame in leaning on family, but always be ready to stand on your own.

## MONEY IN RELATIONSHIPS:
*Joint Accounts, Trust, and Money Disagreements*

Money talks in relationships can go south quickly. You're in love, you're planning for the future, but here's the deal: money isn't romantic. Splitting bills, deciding how to handle joint expenses, and figuring out how to save together takes clear communication—and yes, it can get awkward.

### *JOINT ACCOUNTS: TO MERGE OR NOT TO MERGE?*

At some point in a serious relationship, you'll wonder: Should we open a joint account? My advice? Only if you're both 100% ready. Joint accounts are great for shared expenses (like rent or vacations), but they can be tricky if one person is a spender and the other is a saver.

**Here's how to navigate it:**

◊ **Start small:** If you're not ready to go all-in, open a joint account for specific things, like bills or saving for a trip, while keeping your personal accounts separate.

◊ **Set limits:** Agree on how much each person will contribute to the joint account and what that money will be used for.

**Uncle Aaron's Take:** Love is great and all, but money? That's a whole other commitment. Keep it separate until you're absolutely sure you're ready to mingle finances.

### *HANDLING MONEY FIGHTS IN RELATIONSHIPS:*
### *It's Not About the Math*

Let's get real: money fights aren't really about money. They're about control, security, and sometimes fear. Whether you're splitting bills, saving for a house, or arguing over who's spending too much on takeout, the key is to focus on the underlying issues:

◊ **It's not a blame game:** If one of you overspent this month, don't start pointing fingers. Talk about why it happened and how you can fix it together.

◊ **Have regular money check-ins:** Set aside time (maybe once a month) to talk about your finances together. That way, no one feels blind sided by a money issue that's been brewing under the surface.

### *UNCLE AARON'S GOLDEN RULE OF*
### *RELATIONSHIPS AND MONEY:*

*Talk early, talk often, and always leave room for compromise.*

## FINAL THOUGHTS: BUILDING FINANCIAL TRUST

At the end of the day, money conversations are all about trust and transparency. Whether you're lending a few bucks to a friend or negotiating a salary at work, being open and clear about your financial expectations can save you a world of trouble.

And remember, these conversations are like a muscle—the more you work at them, the stronger (and easier) they get. So go on, flex those financial conversation skills—you've got this!

# 13

## KIDS AND MONEY
## SAVING FOR THEM & TEACHING THEM RIGHT

Alright, let's sit down and talk about something incredibly important—teaching kids about money. I know, money can seem like a dry subject, especially when you're trying to get your kids—whether they're like Lizzy, busy with cheerleading and socializing, Kyle, focused on academics and track, or Nicolas, getting ready to tackle adulthood—to pay attention.

But here's the thing: money management is one of the most valuable life skills you can teach them. It's right up there with learning how to ride a bike or drive a car.

Why? Because whether they realize it or not, how they handle money will impact almost every decision they make as adults—from where they live, what career they pursue, to how they manage their own families someday.

Studies show that financial literacy is alarmingly low among young people. According to a 2021 report from the Council for Economic Education, only 21 states in the U.S. require high school students to take a course in personal finance. This means most young people are entering adulthood without a solid foundation in how to handle money. And get this—70% of teens admit they don't know much about personal finance, according to a survey by Junior Achievement USA.

If your kids don't learn about money from you, chances are they'll pick up bad habits elsewhere—or worse, they'll get a rude awakening when they're faced with real-life financial decisions and aren't prepared. Teaching them early sets them up for success, and trust me, they'll thank you later when they're not stuck in a paycheck-to-paycheck cycle or drowning in debt.

## THE BIG IDEA: MAKE MONEY FUN
*(Even If They Don't Know It Yet)*

When it comes to teaching kids about money, one of the best strategies is to make it engaging and fun—even if they don't realize they're learning something important.

**Let's face it:** if you sit them down and try to explain compound interest or budgeting straight up, you might as well be speaking a foreign language. So instead, get creative.

A 2019 study by the University of Cambridge found that children as young as seven years old start developing money habits. That's right—*seven*. So the earlier you start, the better. But don't worry, even if you have teenagers who roll their eyes every time you bring up finances, it's not too late.

## THE JAR METHOD:
*Teaching Kids About Spending, Saving, and Giving*

One of my favorite techniques to teach kids how to manage money, no matter their age, is the Jar Method. It's simple, visual, and—best of all—it works. I've used this with all three of my kids, and while it took a little nudging at first, they eventually got the hang of it.

**Here's how it works:**

Grab Three Jars, label them; Spend, Save, and Give.

Every time your kids get money—whether it's from an allowance, birthday cash, or money they earned from a summer job—they split it between the jars.

◊ **Spend:** This is their fun money. They can use it on whatever they want, but once it's gone, it's gone. This helps them learn the importance of budgeting for the things they want.

◊ **Save:** This jar teaches them patience and long-term thinking. They can only dip into it when they've reached a savings goal, like buying a new gaming console or cheerleading gear.

◊ **Give:** This jar teaches empathy and charity. It's important for kids to learn that money isn't just for their own benefit—it can help others too.

Studies show that when kids learn about spending, saving, and giving early, they're more likely to make sound financial decisions as adults. And here's the kicker: it's never too early to start.

## THE EVOLUTION OF THE "GIVE" JAR:
*From Charity to Retirement*

Now, the Give jar serves as more than just a way for kids to practice generosity. As they grow into adulthood, that "give" mentality transforms into something even more profound—it becomes about giving back to your future self. In adult life, this mentality is crucial when planning for retirement.

### *So, HOW DOES THE GIVE JAR EVOLVE?*

Simple. As your kids start thinking about the future, the Give jar slowly morphs into the Retirement jar. In a way, by learning to allocate a portion of their money toward giving, they've also been training themselves to put money aside for their future.

Just like giving to charity is about selflessness, contributing to retirement is about self-preservation—thinking long-term and ensuring they're taken care of when they're older.

The Jar Method is a simple, scalable system that starts with allowances and can easily adapt to full salaries, *401(k)s, IRAs, and emergency funds*. The jars will evolve into more sophisticated buckets, but the principles will remain the same.

The Jar Method we started with in childhood now becomes the foundation of a robust financial system in adulthood—one that helps them plan, save, and invest in a balanced way. That's why this method is scalable and evolves with them as they take on bigger responsibilities, from student loans to mortgages to retirement funds.

And guess what? Just as they've learned to set aside money for charity and giving, they've already built the discipline and mindset needed to consistently save for retirement—and that's a gift that keeps on giving.

## COLLEGE FUNDS:
*Saving for the Future, One Dollar at a Time*

Let's switch gears and talk about one of the biggest financial hurdles parents and kids face together—college costs. If you've ever thought about how much college will cost by the time your kids are ready, you've probably broken out in a cold sweat. And for good reason. According to the College Board, the average cost of tuition and fees for the 2023–2024 academic year was about $39,400 at private colleges and $10,560 for in-state students at public universities. That's no small chunk of change.

### *529 COLLEGE SAVINGS PLANS:*
*Your Secret Weapon*

So how do you tackle this mountain of expenses? Enter the 529 Plan—a tax-advantaged savings account specifically designed for education expenses. Here's the deal: the money you put into a 529 plan grows tax-free, and when it's time to pay for tuition, books, or even room and board, you can withdraw it without paying taxes on the earnings.

**Pro Tip: Even small** contributions make a big difference over time thanks to compound interest. If you start putting away **just $50 a month** when your child is born, by the time they're 18, you'll have built up a nice cushion to help cover those hefty tuition bills.

*In fact, with an average annual return of 6-7%, that $50 a month could grow to over $20,000 by the time college rolls around.*

According to Morningstar, families who start saving for college when their child is young can reduce the need for student loans significantly. This means less debt for your kids to carry into their adult lives, giving them a stronger financial foundation from the start.

## TEACHING TEENS ABOUT MONEY:
*Avoiding the Trap of Instant Gratification*

As kids grow into teenagers, their relationship with money becomes more complex. They're dealing with bigger expenses, peer pressure, and—let's face it—the desire for instant gratification. And with the rise of buy-now-pay-later schemes and the allure of credit cards, it's easy for them to fall into bad spending habits.

## CREDIT CARDS AND DEBIT CARDS:
*Lessons in Plastic*

For teens, credit and debit cards can be useful tools to teach financial responsibility, but they have to understand the consequences. Here's what I did with my kids:

◊ I started them off with a prepaid debit card. This way, they could spend what was loaded onto the card, and once it was gone, that was it—no overdraft fees, no surprises.

◊ When they were ready for a credit card, I made sure they understood how interest works and why it's important to pay off the balance every month. This is crucial because misusing credit can lead to debt spirals that are hard to escape from.

Teaching teens to use credit responsibly is like handing them the keys to their financial future. Done right, they'll have a healthy credit score by the time they need to apply for loans or even buy a home.

## SAVING FOR BIG GOALS: TEEN EDITION

You know how I mentioned Nicolas half-listening to my financial advice? Well, one time he actually paid attention—and it paid off. He was saving for a new parts for his car, and instead of blowing all his birthday and part time job money, I helped him set up a savings plan. We wrote out how much he needed to save each month, and when he hit his goal, picked up the parts. Now, he has a car fund and makes monthly purchases. That's the power of goal-setting.

It's the same with any big goal—whether it's a car, a trip, or college expenses. Helping kids set and track goals early helps them understand how savings and delayed gratification work.

They'll be less likely to fall into the instant gratification trap and more likely to make sound financial choices as adults.

### *Uncle Aaron's Christmas Gift Card Hack*

Here's a little trick for holiday shopping: **Buy gift cards throughout the year**. Every time you're at the grocery store or pharmacy, toss in a $10 or $20 gift card. By the time Christmas comes around, you'll have a stash of gift cards ready to give out.

No last-minute stress, no scrambling to find the perfect gift, and—here's the best part—your budget won't take a huge hit all at once. Instead of facing a financial squeeze in December, you'll have slowly built up a holiday fund without even noticing it.

This simple strategy has saved me more times than I care to admit. Plus, by spreading out your gift-buying throughout the year, you're not dipping into your emergency fund or savings goals—a win-win.

## OTHER LITTLE-KNOWN TRICKS TO SAVE BIG

Now, here's where things get interesting. You've probably heard of layaway (yep, it still exists), but did you know there are other sneaky ways to save big with major retailers using price adjustment policies?

Stores like Target and Best Buy will refund you the difference if the price drops on an item you've recently bought. It's basically like free money! Keep an eye on sales, and if you see the price dip after you made your purchase, just ask for a price adjustment.

Many stores have policies that allow for this within a certain timeframe (usually two weeks), and all it takes is a little vigilance.

This isn't just a trick for the holidays—it's a smart move for any big purchase, from electronics to household goods.

These little savings add up over time and help keep your budget in check without having to cut corners.

## TEACHING KIDS ABOUT GIVING:
*Money Isn't Just About Spending*

One of the most valuable lessons you can teach your kids about money is that it's not just for personal gain—it can also be used to help others. Whether it's donating to a charity, sponsoring a family in need during the holidays, or simply giving their time and resources to a cause they care about, teaching kids to give back is essential for their financial education.

**Here's the thing:** involving your kids in the giving process teaches them that money isn't just a tool for accumulating "stuff"—it's a way to make the world a better place. Whether it's through their Give jar or their personal time, showing them how generosity can impact lives is a crucial life skill.

Involve them in the decision-making process. Let them help choose where the Give jar money goes. Do they want to donate to an animal shelter? Help sponsor a child in need? Contribute to a local cause? By giving them some control over where their money goes, you're empowering them to connect their financial decisions to real-world outcomes.

Teaching kids about giving isn't just about charity—it's about showing them that money is a tool for positive change. This lesson will resonate with them as they grow up, helping them develop a more balanced and thoughtful relationship with their finances.

## UNCLE AARON'S FINAL WORD ON TEACHING KIDS ABOUT MONEY

At the end of the day, here's what I've learned: kids are always watching. Whether it's how you manage bills, how you talk about money, or how you save for the future, they're picking up on your habits and mindset around finances. It's essential to be open, honest, and—most importantly—consistent when it comes to teaching them about money. Even if it feels like they're only half-listening (trust me, I've been there with Nicolas and Kyle), they're absorbing more than you think.

Remember, these money lessons aren't a one-time thing. It's an ongoing conversation that evolves as your kids grow. Start with the basics when they're young, and keep adding layers as they get older and more independent. You'll be surprised how much they'll remember when they need it the most—and they'll thank you for it when they're successfully managing their own finances one day.

So whether it's through jars, prepaid debit cards, or those life-saving 529 plans, the goal is the same: *empower your kids to be financially independent, responsible, and smart about their money.* You're setting them up for success, and that's a legacy worth investing in.

## WE COVERED:

◊ **Jar Method:** Introduce spending, saving, and giving at a young age through a simple system that builds lifelong habits.

◊ **The Give Jar's Evolution:** What starts as charity in childhood transforms into retirement planning in adulthood.

◊ **College Savings:** Start small, but start early—with tools like 529 Plans to help minimize future debt.

◊ **Credit & Debit:** Prepaid debit cards and early credit education can lay the foundation for smart spending and strong credit scores.

◊ **Goal Setting:** Help kids save for big-ticket items to teach the power of delayed gratification.

◊ **Shopping Hacks:** From price adjustment policies to spreading out holiday shopping with gift cards, there are smart ways to keep spending in check.

◊ **Giving:** Teach the value of giving—whether through money, time, or resources—so kids develop empathy and understand money's role beyond personal gain.

By planting these seeds early, you're not just raising financially smart kids—you're raising future adults who can handle their money with confidence. They'll take these lessons with them through every stage of life, from their first job to their first house, and all the way to retirement. Now that's a legacy worth leaving behind.

# 14

## PREPARING FOR RETIREMENT
### (EVEN IN YOUR 20S)

Alright, folks, we've arrived at one of the most critical yet least talked-about topics in your financial journey—retirement planning. Now, if you're reading this in your 20s, you're probably thinking, "Retirement? Seriously, Uncle Aaron?

I'm just trying to figure out how to get through the week without burning out or accidentally paying my Netflix subscription twice!" I hear you, loud and clear. But trust me on this one—starting now is the biggest favor you can do for future-you.

It's like planting a tree when you're 20, and by the time you're 50 (or heck, maybe 50 is your preferred retirement date—why not dream big?), you'll be sitting under that shady tree, sipping an iced tea, feeling like a financial genius while everyone else is out there sweating in the sun, working longer than they planned. You'll be watching the world go by, relaxed and retirement-ready, instead of wondering why you didn't start sooner.

So, buckle up, because we're about to dive into the what, why, and how of retirement planning—even if it feels like something that's light years away. Trust me, future-you is already high-fiving you for reading this.

## WHY START PLANNING IN YOUR 20'S?

Imagine this: You start putting aside just $100 a month when you're 25. By the time you hit 65, with an average annual return of 7%, you'd have over $240,000! Now imagine you waited until you were 40 to start. You'd only have about $80,000 by retirement. Time is your biggest ally when it comes to retirement, thanks to the power of compound interest.

### HERE'S AN EXAMPLE TO BLOW YOUR MIND:

If someone had invested $1,000 in the S&P 500 in 1990 and allowed it to grow, compounded yearly based on the actual yearly returns through 2023, your investment would be worth approximately $27,308.33 after 34 years—just the magic of compound interest.

### BUT WAIT, THERE'S MORE!

What if I told you that starting with $25,000 at age 30 and allowed it to grow at an average rate of 7% annually in a low-cost index fund, by age 65, your investment would grow to approximately $266,914.54 Yep, that's real. The earlier you start, the better off you'll be.

## YOUR RETIREMENT TOOLBOX:
*401(k)s, IRAs, and More*

Now, let's talk tools. The great thing about retirement is that there are several ways to get there, each with its own perks and quirks. Let's go over the most common options for building your retirement nest egg.

### *401(K)S: THE CLASSIC OPTION*

If you've got a job with benefits, there's a good chance you've heard of a 401(k). It's like the holy grail of employer-sponsored retirement accounts. You contribute pre-tax dollars from your paycheck, and the money grows tax-deferred until you withdraw it at retirement.

**Here's why 401(k)s rock:**

◊ Employer Matching: Many companies will match a portion of your contributions. It's free money! Think of it as a bonus for saving for your future.

◊ Tax Benefits: Contributions are made pre-tax, which lowers your taxable income now. The money grows tax-deferred, meaning you don't pay taxes on it until you withdraw it in retirement.

One thing to watch out for, though, is 401(k) fees. Be sure you understand what your plan charges you to manage your investments. A 1% fee might not sound like much, but over 30 years, it can eat up thousands of dollars in your savings.

**If your employer** offers a match, contribute enough to get that full match—never leave free money on the table!

### *IRAS: TRADITIONAL VS. ROTH*

If you don't have a 401(k), or you want to contribute more than what's allowed, enter the IRA—the Individual Retirement Account. There are two main types: Traditional and Roth IRAs. Here's the scoop on both:

◊ **Traditional IRA:** You contribute pre-tax dollars, and your money grows tax-deferred until you withdraw it at retirement. You'll pay taxes on the withdrawals, but since you're likely to be in a lower tax bracket when you retire, this can work out in your favor.

◊ **Roth IRA:** This one's a bit different. You contribute after-tax dollars, so you won't get a tax break now, but your money grows tax-free, and you won't pay taxes when you withdraw it at retirement. For young folks, a Roth IRA is a fantastic option because your income (and therefore your tax rate) is likely lower now than it will be later.

**Uncle Aaron's Tip**: A Roth IRA can be your best friend in your 20s and 30s. It's like planting a garden that grows tax-free forever!

## THE FIRE MOVEMENT:
*Financial Independence, Retire Early*

Now let's talk about something that's been trending: the FIRE movement. This isn't just about retiring at 65—it's about retiring way earlier by being smart, frugal, and intentional about saving. FIRE advocates aim to retire as early as their 30s or 40s by saving aggressively (sometimes up to 50% or more of their income) and living off investments.

While FIRE isn't for everyone (let's be real, it's hard to save 50% of your income if you're living in a big city or have a family), the principles of aggressive saving and investing early are solid. The key takeaway from FIRE is to live below your means and invest wisely.

## INDEXED UNIVERSAL LIFE INSURANCE (IUL):
*A Retirement Plan with Growth Potential*

Okay, let's get into something that doesn't get talked about enough: Indexed Universal Life Insurance (IUL). This is an insurance product, but it's also a sneaky-good retirement strategy.

An IUL combines life insurance with an investment component tied to a stock market index (like the S&P 500).

The cool part? Your cash value can grow based on stock market performance, but it's protected from losses if the market tanks. It's like having a safety net for your retirement funds.

**Here's how it works:**

◊ You pay your premiums (which cover the insurance and investment portions).

◊ The cash value grows over time, tax-deferred, and is linked to an index like the S&P 500.

◊ You can access this cash in retirement, often tax-free, making it a solid supplement to your other retirement accounts.

**If you want a mix** of growth potential and protection, an IUL might be a great addition to your retirement strategy—especially if you like the idea of tax-free withdrawals down the road.

## ROLLOVERS:
*Moving Your Money When You Change Jobs*

So, you're 28, you've switched jobs a few times, and now you've got little chunks of 401(k) money scattered all over the place. What do you do? You roll it over into an IRA.

**Here's why this matters:**

◊ **No More Fees:** Many employers charge fees to maintain your 401(k) after you leave. Rolling over your 401(k) into an IRA means you're in control of your money and can usually lower those fees.

◊ **More Control:** With an IRA, you can invest in almost anything—stocks, bonds, index funds, you name it. You're not limited to the options your employer chose for you.

## DIVORCE AND RETIREMENT:
*Splitting the Nest Egg*

Now, let's get real for a second. Life doesn't always go as planned, and divorce can throw a wrench in your financial game. But here's something most people don't realize: retirement accounts are considered marital property, which means they can be split during a divorce.

This is where something called a QDRO (*Qualified Domestic Relations Order*) comes in. It allows you to split your 401(k) or pension without triggering taxes or penalties.

If you're the one receiving the funds, you can roll them into an IRA and let that money keep growing until retirement.

Also, keep in mind that some couples divide IRAs in divorce settlements. When done right, you can split an IRA without paying taxes or penalties, as long as the transfer is done via divorce decree.

**If you're going t**hrough a divorce, make sure your attorney understands the financial side of things, particularly how to handle retirement assets. And yes, I've been through it—I know firsthand how important it is to have a solid plan.

## 1031 EXCHANGES:
*Swapping Properties Without Taxes*

Another tool in your long-term wealth-building kit is the 1031 exchange. If you're in the real estate game, this is a way to defer capital gains taxes by "swapping" one investment property for another. This strategy can be super effective for building wealth through real estate, but it's also tricky, so make sure you've got a tax professional on your side.

**In a nutshell, here's how it works:**

- ◊ You sell one investment property and reinvest the proceeds in a like-kind property (another investment property).

- ◊ By doing this, you defer paying capital gains taxes until you sell the new property (hopefully, at an even higher price later on).

**Real estate can b**e a powerful way to build wealth, but navigating the tax side requires professional help. That's where a CPA or financial advisor comes in.

## FINAL THOUGHTS: START EARLY, STAY CONSISTENT

The bottom line? Time is your friend. Whether you're investing in a 401(k), IRA, or even an IUL, starting early gives your money decades to grow. The key is consistency—keep contributing, no matter how small, and avoid dipping into your savings before retirement. And don't be afraid to call in the pros—a financial advisor can help you maximize your options and avoid costly mistakes.

**The earlier you s**tart saving, the better. But even if you're late to the game, don't sweat it—there are always ways to get back on track. Get some help if you need it. Your future self is already thanking you!

## WHAT WE COVERED:

We dug into retirement planning—why it's important, how to use 401(k)s and IRAs, and why starting early makes all the difference. Spoiler: the earlier you start, the easier retirement will be.

### *WHAT I WANT YOU TO REMEMBER:*

*The best time to start saving for retirement was yesterday. The second-best time is today. Even small contributions now will grow into something big by the time you're ready to retire.*

## UNCLE AARON'S ACTION PLAN:

◊ Contribute to Your 401(k): If your employer offers a match, take it—it's free money!

◊ Open a Roth IRA: If you don't have a 401(k), start a Roth IRA and make regular contributions.

◊ Set a Retirement Savings Goal: Use a calculator to figure out how much you'll need to retire comfortably.

# PART 5:

## ADVANCED WEALTH STRATEGIES

*Uncle Aaron's Guide to Playing Chess, Not Checkers*

Alright, folks, we've budgeted, saved, and hustled like pros, but now it's time to stop playing checkers and start thinking like chess masters. Welcome to the big leagues of wealth-building, where the moves you make today can shape your future for years to come. This isn't about nickel-and-diming your way to riches—it's about pulling off the kind of power plays that will have future-you kicking back on a beach, wondering why it took so long to start.

In this part, we're talking next-level moves: how to avoid the big financial traps, how to negotiate like a boss, and how to make Uncle Sam work for you (hello, taxes!).

These are the strategies that separate the wealthy from the "wealthy on Instagram." So buckle up, because it's time to learn the game-changing tactics that'll turn your financial dreams into reality. And trust me, once you're in this mindset, there's no going back.

Ready to up your wealth game? Let's make it happen!

# 15

## FINANCIAL PITFALLS TO AVOID

Alright, let's talk about what not to do with your money. Because no matter how much you've read, or how many Uncle Aaron pep talks you've had, you'll face financial traps along the way. It's part of the game, but avoiding these pitfalls is what separates the financially savvy from the flat-out broke.

Let's be real—being a young adult with access to credit cards, shiny gadgets, and all the latest apps can make overspending feel almost inevitable. And that's where the first major pitfall comes in…

**OVERSPENDING ON CREDIT:**
*The Silent Wallet Killer*

Ah, credit cards. Those sleek pieces of plastic feel like magic when you swipe, but they come with a big catch. Credit cards aren't evil by themselves—in fact, they can be fantastic tools for building credit, getting rewards, and covering emergencies. But if you treat them like free money, they'll quickly morph into the monsters of debt.

One missed payment, and you're hit with interest charges that make it harder to pay off the balance. Before you know it, you're drowning in minimum payments, and that new pair of sneakers? They just cost you twice what you thought.

**Here's the thing**—credit cards are like chainsaws. Super useful, but also super dangerous if you're not careful. You wouldn't start chopping wood without knowing how to handle the saw, right? Same goes for credit cards.

Always, always pay off the full balance each month. And if you can't, don't charge more than you can handle. Debt isn't just a number on a bill—it's a chain that can drag you down faster than you can say "APR."

## LIFESTYLE INFLATION:
*When You Start Living Beyond Your Means*

Remember when you got your first real paycheck, and you thought, "I'm rolling in cash!"? Maybe you upgraded your phone, splurged on dinners out, or finally bought those concert tickets.

That's lifestyle inflation creeping in, my friend. The more you make, the more you spend—until you're living paycheck to paycheck despite earning more than you ever have. It's sneaky because it feels like you're just "treating yourself," but in reality, it's a recipe for financial stress.

### *SPOTTING THE TRAP*

Lifestyle inflation happens when you start spending money on wants as if they were needs. Sure, you can afford the $4 latte every day now, but do you need it?

The key is to remember that just because your income has increased doesn't mean your spending should follow suit. Your focus should be on saving that extra cash, not blowing it on the latest gadgets or subscriptions.

**I tell my son this** all the time: *"Just because you've got a raise doesn't mean you need a fancier life."* Take that extra money and invest it or stash it in savings for a rainy day. You'll thank me when you're not scrambling for cash later on when life throws you a curveball (which it will).

## PAYDAY LOANS:
*The Debt Trap with a Smile*

Imagine this: You're broke, and payday's a week away, but your car breaks down. You see a payday loan shop, and the ad says they'll give you cash instantly—sounds great, right? Nope. Payday loans are the ultimate debt trap. These loans come with absurdly high interest rates, sometimes as much as 400%. You borrow $500, and before you know it, you owe twice that. It's like borrowing from a mob boss—you'll never dig yourself out.

### WHY THEY'RE SO DANGEROUS.

◊ Payday loans are marketed as quick fixes, but they come with brutal fees and interest rates that trap you in a cycle of debt.

◊ Many people end up having to take out more loans just to cover the original payday loan. It's a vicious cycle that can destroy your finances before you even realize what's happening.

**Avoid payday loan**s like the plague. If you're in a tight spot, consider other options first—ask family for help, sell something, or even use a credit card if you have to.

Payday loans should always be a last resort because they're the fast track to financial ruin.

## RED FLAGS IN CONTRACTS:
*The Fine Print You Can't Ignore*

Whether it's a rental agreement, a car loan, or even your cell phone plan, contracts are everywhere. And let me tell you, those long paragraphs of legal jargon are there for a reason—and it's not to protect you. Companies bank on the fact that you won't read the fine print, which often hides sneaky fees, automatic renewals, or crazy interest rates.

**How to Spot Red Flags:**

When you're signing any kind of contract, always look for the following:

◊ **Hidden Fees:** Some contracts will sneak in fees for things like early termination, maintenance, or service changes. These can add up quickly.

◊ **Interest Rate Changes:** Some loans have variable interest rates, meaning they can skyrocket after a certain period, leaving you with higher payments than expected.

◊ **Automatic Renewals:** Watch out for contracts that renew automatically without giving you a heads-up—this is especially common with gym memberships and subscription services.

◊ **Balloon Payments:** Some loans have a "balloon payment" at the end, where you're hit with a massive lump sum that you'll need to pay all at once. Always know what your long-term financial commitment looks like.

**If the contract** looks like something that could knock you over the head later, run it by someone who knows their stuff.

A financial advisor, a lawyer, or even just someone who's been around the block a few times (yep, that's me). It's always better to ask questions now than be surprised later.

## STUDENT LOANS:
*The Long Road to Payback*

Ah, student loans—the necessary evil for many who want that degree but don't have a trust fund. While getting an education is one of the best investments you can make, not all loans are created equal. Some have grace periods, fixed rates, and decent terms. Others? Not so much. The key is understanding the terms before you sign that dotted line.

**The Two Main Types:**

◊ **Federal Loans:** These are typically the better option, with fixed interest rates, income-driven repayment plans, and opportunities for forgiveness programs. They're a lifesaver for many, but they still require careful management to avoid ballooning interest.

◊ **Private Loans:** If you've maxed out your federal loans, you might be tempted to grab a private loan. Be cautious—these loans often come with higher interest rates, less flexible repayment options, and far fewer protections.

**When it comes to** student loans, aim to borrow only what you really need.

It's tempting to take out more than you require for that lifestyle upgrade (hello, fancy off-campus apartment), but remember: you'll be paying it back with interest.

And if you can swing it, pay more than the minimum payment each month. This will help you knock down that debt faster and save you a boatload of cash in the long run.

## THE POWER OF DEBT SNOWBALL
*and Twice-a-Month Payments*

Paying off debt is like chipping away at an iceberg. But there's a strategy for that—the debt snowball method. You start by paying off your smallest debts first, gaining momentum as each balance hits zero.

The psychological win keeps you motivated, and as your smaller debts disappear, you'll have more cash to throw at the bigger ones.

**Another strategy?**

Twice-a-month payments. Instead of making just one payment at the end of the month, split it into two payments every two weeks.

This simple trick reduces the amount of interest that piles up on your balance over time. You'll knock down your debt faster without feeling like you're making massive sacrifices.

**Debt is like quic**ksand—if you only make the minimum payments, you'll barely make a dent.

But if you're smart about it, you can dig yourself out way sooner than you'd expect. Pick one debt, attack it with everything you've got, then move on to the next one. You'll be debt-free before you know it.

## LOAN FORGIVENESS:
*What You Need to Know in 2024*

If you're dealing with student loans, you've probably heard whispers about loan forgiveness. It's not a myth—but it's not a magic solution either. Loan forgiveness programs, especially for federal loans, are available for those who meet specific criteria, like working in public service or making consistent payments under an income-driven repayment plan for a certain number of years.

**But here's the deal:** eligibility and requirements change, and not everyone will qualify. It's crucial to stay updated on the latest forgiveness policies, especially as new changes roll out in 2024.

Don't just assume your debt will disappear—make sure you're following the right steps to qualify.

**Stay on top of yo**ur loans, and don't rely on forgiveness programs as your only strategy.

They can help, but they shouldn't be your entire plan for paying off debt. If you can, start paying more than the minimum now. Future you will be so grateful.

In the end, avoiding financial pitfalls is about staying informed, knowing your options, and having a plan. Whether it's steering clear of bad debt, avoiding payday loans, or making strategic payments on your student loans, it all comes down to making smart choices now that will set you up for success later.

**And trust me—ther**e's nothing better than that feeling of knowing you've got control of your money, instead of the other way around.

# 16

## CREDIT BUILDING AND REPAIRING

Alright, let's talk about something that feels like a mysterious secret to many young adults—your credit score. It's that magical number that can make or break your financial opportunities. But here's the kicker: most people don't even think about their credit score until they need it for something important, like buying a car, renting an apartment, or applying for a loan. And trust me, when you're staring at that number and it's lower than you expected, it's a bit like finding out your favorite pizza place is closed after a long day. A real bummer.

But don't sweat it—building and repairing your credit isn't some mystical process only gurus understand. It's actually pretty straightforward, as long as you know what to do (and what to avoid). So, grab a snack and get ready for Uncle Aaron's no-nonsense guide to credit.

## WHAT'S A CREDIT SCORE?

Let's start with the basics. Your credit score is a three-digit number that tells lenders how likely you are to pay back money you borrow. Think of it like a financial report card.

The higher the score, the more likely lenders are to see you as trustworthy, which means you'll get better deals on loans, credit cards, and other financial products. It's a bit like being on the honor roll—good credit equals perks.

### *How is Your Credit Score Calculated?*

Your credit score is based on several key factors that give lenders insight into how you handle your financial responsibilities. Let's break it down into digestible bites:

◊ **Payment History (35%):** This is the big one. It's like your attendance record in school—are you consistently showing up on time? In credit terms, it means, are you making your payments on time? Even one late payment can tank your score, so consistency is crucial.

◊ **Credit Utilization (30%):** This refers to how much of your available credit you're using. For example, if you have a $1,000 credit limit and you've charged $500, your credit utilization rate is 50%. Ideally, you want to keep this number below 30%. Why? Because maxing out your credit cards makes you look financially strained, and lenders don't love that.

◊ **Length of Credit History (15%):** The longer you've had credit, the better. This is like being the responsible kid who's been in the class for years. Lenders want to see that you can handle credit over time.

◊ **New Credit Inquiries (10%):** Every time you apply for new credit (like a loan or credit card), it results in a "hard inquiry" on your report. Too many of these in a short period can make you look desperate for credit, which raises a red flag for lenders.

◊ **Credit Mix (10%):** Lenders like to see a good variety of credit types, such as credit cards, student loans, and maybe even a mortgage one day. It shows you can manage different forms of credit responsibly.

**Think of your cre**dit score like a plant. You've got to water it (by paying your bills on time), prune it (by keeping your credit utilization low), and give it time to grow (by holding onto your accounts for years). It's not a sprint—it's a marathon.

## BUILDING CREDIT FROM SCRATCH

So, you're starting with no credit history. That's okay! Everyone starts somewhere. Building credit takes time, but there are some easy ways to get started.

### GET A SECURED CREDIT CARD

A secured credit card is one of the easiest ways to build credit when you're just starting out. You put down a deposit (usually $200 or so), and that becomes your credit limit. Use it just like any other credit card—buy stuff, pay it off on time, and watch your score slowly build.

The beauty of secured credit cards is that they report to the credit bureaus just like a regular credit card, so you're building your credit with every responsible swipe. Eventually, you'll be able to upgrade to an unsecured card and get your deposit back.

### BECOME AN AUTHORIZED USER

If you've got a responsible family member (hint: this is where parents or older siblings come in handy) with a credit card, ask if you can become an authorized user. This means their good credit behavior will reflect positively on your credit report, helping you build credit without even using the card yourself.

### *CREDIT BUILDER LOANS*

Some banks and credit unions offer credit builder loans specifically designed to help people establish credit. These loans work a bit differently—you borrow a small amount, but the money is held in a savings account while you make payments. Once you've paid off the loan, you get access to the funds, and your timely payments boost your credit score.

**Credit isn't buil**t overnight. It takes time, patience, and consistency. But once you start seeing that score tick up, you'll feel like a boss. Trust me, future-you is going to love looking back and knowing you made the right moves.

## REPAIRING A BAD CREDIT SCORE

So, maybe you've had a few slip-ups. Late payments, missed bills, or maybe you got in over your head with credit card debt. Don't worry—you're not doomed to bad credit forever. The good news is that you can fix it. The bad news? It'll take some time and discipline.

### *CHECK YOUR CREDIT REPORT*

Start by pulling your credit report. You're entitled to a free report from each of the three major credit bureaus—Equifax, Experian, and TransUnion—once a year. Look through it carefully to make sure everything is accurate. If you spot any errors (like a late payment that wasn't actually late), dispute it immediately.

### *PAY OFF DEBT STRATEGICALLY*

If you've got multiple credit cards or loans, the best way to pay them off is by using the debt snowball method. Focus on paying off the smallest balance first, while making minimum payments on everything else. Once the smallest debt is paid off, move to the next one, and so on. It creates momentum and helps you feel more in control.

Alternatively, there's the debt avalanche method, where you focus on paying off the highest-interest debt first. This will save you more money in the long run, but it takes longer to see those smaller balances disappear.

### *NEGOTIATE WITH CREDITORS*

If you're really struggling, it's worth calling your creditors and negotiating. They may offer you a lower interest rate, a payment plan, or even settle for less than what you owe. Just make sure to get any agreements in writing.

### *AVOID CLOSING OLD ACCOUNTS*

You might be tempted to close credit card accounts once they're paid off, but don't do it. Remember, your length of credit history is a factor in your score. Keeping those accounts open (even with a zero balance) can help boost your score over time.

**Don't try to fix** everything at once—it'll just stress you out. Instead, focus on one thing at a time. Pay off one debt, clean up one area of your report, and before you know it, your score will start creeping back up.

## WHY CREDIT SCORES MATTER
*(More Than You Think)*

Sure, a good credit score helps you get better deals on loans and credit cards, but that's just the beginning.

Here's why your credit score matters more than you might realize:

◊ **Renting an Apartment:** Landlords often check your credit score to make sure you're a responsible tenant. A bad score could mean getting denied for that dream apartment.

◊ **Getting a Job:** Some employers (especially in finance or jobs that handle money) check your credit report as part of the hiring process. It's not fair, but it happens.

◊ **Lower Interest Rates:** The better your score, the lower your interest rates on loans, mortgages, and even some credit cards. A lower rate can save you thousands over time.

◊ **Insurance Premiums:** Believe it or not, your credit score can even affect your car insurance premiums. A higher score can get you better rates because insurers see you as less risky.

**Think of your credit** score as your financial reputation. It's not just about borrowing money—it affects where you live, what kind of car you drive, and even your job opportunities.

So take care of it like you would your best pair of sneakers—because when it's trashed, it's hard to get it back in shape.

## CREDIT REPAIR SCAMS:
*Avoiding the Pitfalls*

Let's be real—there are a lot of shady companies out there claiming they can "fix" your credit overnight.

**Spoiler alert: they can't.** There's no quick fix for bad credit, and any company that says otherwise is trying to scam you. They'll charge you crazy fees, but you'll be left in the same situation (if not worse).

**How to Spot a Credit Repair Scam:**

◊ **They Ask for Payment Upfront:** Legitimate credit repair services won't ask you to pay before they've done anything.

◊ **They Promise to Erase Legitimate Debt:** No one can remove accurate information from your credit report—if they say they can, run the other way.

◊ **They Guarantee a Specific Credit Score:** No one can guarantee a credit score improvement. It's all based on your actions.

**If your credit's** in rough shape, you don't need some shady company to fix it for you. You can repair it yourself by following the steps we've talked about. Just stay patient, stick with it, and you'll see results.

## THE POWER OF TWICE-A-MONTH PAYMENTS

Now, here's a little secret trick that can make a big difference—twice-a-month payments. Instead of making one payment on your credit card bill each month, split it into **two smaller payments.**

By doing this, you keep your credit utilization lower throughout the month, which can boost your score.

For example, if you have a $1,000 credit limit and you charge $500, your utilization rate is 50%. But if you pay off $250 before the end of the billing cycle, your utilization drops to 25%, and that looks a whole lot better to credit bureaus.

**Credit card companies** don't expect you to pay your bill off multiple times a month, but it's a sneaky way to make sure your utilization stays low. It's like running the dishwasher twice instead of letting dirty dishes pile up—it keeps things clean and manageable.

## UNCLE AARON'S TAKEAWAY:

Building and maintaining good credit is a marathon, not a sprint. Whether you're just starting out or trying to repair the damage, it's all about making smart, consistent choices. Don't get overwhelmed by the numbers or the process—focus on what you can control, take it one step at a time, and before you know it, you'll be in control of your credit and your financial future.

# 17

## TAXES FOR BEGINNERS

Alright, buckle up, because we're about to dive into one of the most dreaded adult responsibilities: taxes. Yeah, I know—just hearing the word probably makes you want to crawl back under the covers or distract yourself with just about anything else.

But here's the thing: understanding taxes is crucial if you want to make smart financial decisions. Think of it like learning the rules of a game. Once you know how to play, you can start winning—and even keep more of your hard-earned cash.

Uncle Aaron's here to make this as painless as possible, with a few laughs along the way. So grab a cup of coffee (or something stronger if this already stresses you out), and let's break down taxes the Uncle Aaron way—simple, relatable, and hopefully a little less overwhelming.

### WHAT ARE TAXES, ANYWAY?

In a nutshell, taxes are the money we pay to the government so they can keep things running—schools, roads, public services, national defense, all that good stuff. Think of it as paying the membership fee for being part of society. Yeah, it stings a little, but it keeps everything from potholes to public libraries running smoothly. Whether we like it or not, taxes are here to stay, so the sooner you get comfortable with the process, the better.

**But here's the good news:** filing taxes doesn't have to be a nightmare. You just need to know the basics, and that's where Uncle Aaron comes in. Let's break it down, starting with the tax forms you'll likely come across and how to make sure you get the most out of your tax return.

"**Think of taxes** like a yearly financial check-up. It might be a little uncomfortable, but in the long run, it keeps your financial life in good shape. And hey, sometimes, you even get a refund—it's like a bonus paycheck."

## UNDERSTANDING YOUR PAYSTUB:
*FICA, Social Security, and Medicare*

Before we jump into tax forms, let's talk about something that confuses a lot of people: your paystub. You've probably noticed that every time you get a paycheck, a chunk of your money gets taken out before it even hits your bank account. You might be wondering, "Where is all that money going?" Well, here's the breakdown of the usual suspects:

◊ **FICA:** This stands for the *Federal Insurance Contributions Act*, and it's the money taken out of your paycheck for Social Security and Medicare. Basically, you're contributing to programs that will (hopefully) benefit you later in life.

◊ **Social Security:** This tax funds retirement, disability, and survivorship benefits. It's about 6.2% of your income, up to a certain limit. Uncle Aaron's advice? "It's like putting a little something away for your older self—kind of like a retirement piggy bank."

◊ **Medicare:** This tax helps fund health coverage for people 65 and older or those with disabilities. It's around 1.45% of your income. "Think of this as future-you's health insurance," Uncle Aaron says.

Together, Social Security and Medicare take about 7.65% of your paycheck (with your employer matching that amount), and that's what you see under FICA on your paystub.

**"When you see FIC**A on your paystub, don't panic—it's not some mysterious black hole sucking up your cash.

That's your contribution to Social Security and Medicare, which, in theory, you'll benefit from down the road. It's kinda like paying it forward to your future self."

## UNDERSTANDING TAX FORMS:
*W-2s, 1099s, and More*

Now that you've got a grip on your paystub, let's talk about the tax forms you'll need when it comes time to file your taxes. If you've ever worked a job or earned money on the side, you've probably heard of some of these forms. Let's break them down:

### W-2

The Classic This is the tax form most people are familiar with. If you have a traditional job where you get a regular paycheck, your employer will send you a W-2 at the end of the year. This form shows how much money you made and how much tax was already taken out of your paycheck for federal, state, and Social Security taxes.

Think of the W-2 as a receipt for your work. It makes filing your taxes easier because all the information is laid out for you. Just plug those numbers into your tax return, and you're golden.

### *1099*

The Gig Economy's Best Frenemy If you've got a side hustle, freelance gig, or any non-traditional job, you'll likely get a 1099 form instead of a W-2. Unlike a W-2, there are no taxes automatically taken out of the money you earn, which means it's your responsibility to handle that. Yeah, it sounds like a pain, but it's manageable. If you earn over $600 from a single client or gig, they're supposed to send you a 1099 at the end of the year.

**"This form is bas**ically saying, 'Congrats on being your own boss—now go figure out your taxes!'"

### *1099-K AND 1099-NEC:*

For Gig Workers and Online Sellers Let's say you're making money selling on Etsy or driving for Uber.

Platforms like these will send you a 1099-K or 1099-NEC if you hit certain income thresholds. These forms report income from third-party transactions or self-employment, and you need to report this income when filing your taxes.

### *W-4*

Getting Your Withholding Right When you start a new job, your employer will give you a W-4 form to fill out. This form tells them how much tax to withhold from your paycheck.

Too little withheld? You could owe money at tax time. Too much? You get a refund, but that means you've been giving the government an interest-free loan all year.

**"It's like buying** coffee every day. You can either pay for it as you go, or wait 'til the end of the year and pay for it all at once. Either way, you're gonna pay—might as well budget for it."

## FILING TAXES: THE PROCESS, SIMPLIFIED

Filing your taxes isn't as complicated as it sounds. Thanks to modern technology, you can use online tax software (like TurboTax, H&R Block, or TaxSlayer) to make things a whole lot easier. Here's how the process typically goes:

### *GATHER YOUR DOCUMENTS*

Before you start filing, make sure you've got everything you need. This includes your W-2 (if you have one), 1099 forms, bank statements, and receipts for any tax-deductible expenses like student loan interest or charitable donations.

Trust me, staying organized makes the whole process a breeze.

### *CHOOSE A FILING METHOD*

There are a few ways to file your taxes. If your financial situation is simple (like just a W-2 from one job), you can file for free through IRS Free File.

If you've got a more complex situation (freelance income, investments, etc.), tax software like TurboTax will walk you through it step by step. You could also work with a CPA or tax professional, especially if you're feeling lost.

### *STANDARD DEDUCTION VS. ITEMIZING*

The next big decision is whether to take the standard deduction or itemize your deductions.

**The standard deduction** is a flat amount the government lets you subtract from your income to lower your taxable income. For single filers, it's around $13,850 in 2024. Most people opt for this because it's simple.

**Itemizing** is where you list specific deductions (like mortgage interest, medical expenses, charitable donations, etc.). You should only itemize if your total deductions add up to more than the standard deduction.

**"If you don't own** a home or have significant medical expenses, the standard deduction is probably your best bet. It's quicker, easier, and works well for most people."

### *FILE ONLINE*
#### *(And Get Your Refund Faster)*

Once everything is squared away, submit your tax return electronically (e-file). Not only is it faster, but it's also more accurate, and you'll get your refund sooner if you're owed one.

If you're expecting a refund, you can have it direct-deposited right into your bank account—easy peasy.

### *UNCLE AARON'S STORY OF TAX REGRET:*

**"Back in the day,** I tried to do my taxes the old-fashioned way—pen, paper, and a whole lot of confusion. Long story short, I missed some key deductions, didn't fill out my forms correctly, and ended up owing more than I should've. Don't be like past Uncle Aaron—use the technology we've got now, and keep more of your hard-earned money."

## TAXES AND THE GIG ECONOMY:
*What You Need to Know*

More people than ever are earning money from side hustles, freelancing, and gig work. But here's the catch—if you're your own boss, you're also responsible for setting aside money for taxes. That's because no one is withholding taxes for you like they would with a regular job.

### SELF-EMPLOYMENT TAX

If you earn more than $400 from gig work or freelancing in a year, you're responsible for paying self-employment tax. This covers Social Security and Medicare taxes that would normally be taken out of your paycheck if you were an employee. It's about 15.3% of your income—yeah, I know, it's a chunk. But it's better to know about it upfront than to be hit with a big tax bill later.

### ESTIMATED QUARTERLY PAYMENTS

Since no one's withholding taxes from your side hustle income, you're expected to make quarterly estimated tax payments throughout the year. If you don't, the IRS might slap you with a penalty when you file your taxes.

Pro tip? Set aside at least 25-30% of your side hustle earnings for taxes. You don't want to be caught off guard at tax time with a hefty bill.

**"If you're making** decent money from a side gig, set up a separate savings account just for taxes. Every time you get paid, transfer a percentage into that account. When it's time to make those quarterly payments, you won't be scrambling to come up with the cash."

## DEDUCTIONS, WRITE-OFFS, AND CREDITS:
*Your Tax Lifesavers*

Now, here's the fun part about taxes—yes, I said fun! While paying taxes might feel like a drag, deductions and credits are here to help you lower your tax bill. The government offers all sorts of ways to save if you know where to look. Let's go over some of the most common ones for young adults and side hustlers:

### STUDENT LOAN INTEREST DEDUCTION

If you're paying off student loans, you can deduct up to $2,500 in interest payments from your taxable income. It's a little silver lining for anyone dealing with student loan debt. Just make sure you have your Form 1098-E, which shows how much interest you paid.

### BUSINESS EXPENSES

If you're freelancing or running a side hustle, you can deduct business-related expenses like equipment, software, office supplies, and even part of your rent or utilities if you work from home (hello, home office deduction). Keep those receipts!

"Anything you spend to keep your business running? That could be a write-off. You don't need to be a tax genius, but keep track of every penny, and make sure you're getting those deductions."

### EARNED INCOME TAX CREDIT (EITC)

If you're a low- to moderate-income earner, the EITC is a tax credit designed to put more money back in your pocket. Unlike deductions, tax credits directly reduce the amount of tax you owe, which means you might get a bigger refund.

### EDUCATION CREDITS

Are you in school or paying for classes to further your education? The Lifetime Learning Credit and the American Opportunity Credit are designed to help with the costs of tuition, fees, and other education expenses.

**"If you're invest**ing in yourself through education, you're not just growing your mind—you're saving on taxes, too. Win-win."

## TAX-TIME STRESS RELIEF: KEEP IT SIMPLE

Look, taxes can feel overwhelming, but they don't have to be. The key is to stay organized, know which forms apply to you, and understand how to maximize your deductions and credits.

**Here's Uncle Aaron's biggest piece of advice:** keep good records. Whether you're working a regular job or side hustling, make sure you've got a system to track your income and expenses.

And if you're feeling lost? Don't be afraid to reach out to a tax professional. They're worth every penny if it means avoiding costly mistakes.

## UNCLE AARON'S TAKEAWAY:

"Taxes are like getting a shot at the doctor's office. You dread it, but once it's done, you feel a little relief. Keep good records, stay on top of your payments, and make the most of the deductions and credits you qualify for. And when in doubt? Call a pro—they're there to help."

# 18

## Behavioral Finance and Money Mindset

### REVISITING THE MONEY MINDSET

Remember back in Chapter 2, we talked about how emotions can sneak into your money decisions, often when you least expect them? Whether it's FOMO pushing you to buy that $200 jacket you saw on Instagram or the stress of avoiding your bank balance like the plague, emotions have a way of messing with even the best-laid financial plans.

But knowing that your mind can mess with your money decisions is just the first step. Now, we're going to dive deeper and explore how you can manage those emotions and build a strong, confident money mindset that supports your long-term financial goals.

Enter Maya. She's a 27-year-old marketing professional living in Chicago, juggling a thriving career, student loans, and the pressure of maintaining an Instagram-worthy lifestyle. Maya's got big dreams, but like many young professionals, she faces a few financial hurdles along the way. Fortunately for her, she's got a little help from Uncle Aaron, who she met when he went back to college at the ripe young age of 48 (because yes, lifelong learning is a thing, even at 54).

They took a few marketing courses together, and Maya quickly realized Uncle Aaron wasn't just there to learn—he was a walking encyclopedia of financial advice and life lessons. Ever since, they've stayed in touch, with Maya leaning on him for guidance when her financial stress started to feel a little overwhelming.

So, with Maya's story and Uncle Aaron's tried-and-true wisdom, we're going to explore how you can shift your financial mindset, manage emotional triggers, and start taking control of your financial journey.

## THE PSYCHOLOGY BEHIND MODERN FINANCIAL STRESS

Before we get into strategies, let's talk about why Maya—and probably you—feel stressed about money. It's not just about paying bills anymore. For Millennials and Gen Z (Maya's generation), money is tied to identity, success, and social status. Your financial situation isn't just about what's in your bank account—it's wrapped up in how you perceive yourself and how others perceive you.

According to a 2021 study by the American Psychological Association, 72% of Millennials and 81% of Gen Zers report being stressed about money. Those are some serious numbers, and Uncle Aaron, of course, has thoughts: "That's not just a statistic, that's a financial crisis. If I had a nickel for every young person stressed about student loans, I'd have... well, probably enough to pay off a student loan or two!"

For Maya, financial anxiety comes from a few key places:

1. **Student Loans:** Maya graduated with a marketing degree—

and a pile of student debt. Even though she's got a good job at a Chicago firm, her monthly student loan payments loom like a dark cloud. "It's like no matter how much I make, those loans are always there, reminding me of what I still owe," she says.

**Uncle Aaron quips**, "Ah, student loans. I remember the days when you could work a summer job and pay off a year's tuition. Now, they give you a diploma and a bill that might as well be written in blood. But hey, it's all part of the ride, right?"

2. **Big-City Living:** Chicago's not cheap. Between rent, utilities, transportation, and the ever-present temptation of the city's restaurant scene, Maya's paycheck disappears fast. "In a place like Chicago, you pay for the lifestyle, not just the rent," Uncle Aaron reminds her. "But a savvy city slicker like Maya? She's figuring it out."

3. **Social Pressure:** Social media is full of influencers living their best lives—vacations, luxury shopping, brunch every weekend. Maya sees it all and feels the pressure to keep up. "I know it's not real life," she admits, "but sometimes I feel like I'm the only one sitting at home while everyone else is out there living."

**"Trust me, kid, h**alf those people are probably eating ramen noodles between their fancy brunches."

## COMMON EMOTIONAL TRIGGERS
*in Financial Decision-Making*

Alright, so we know that emotions can mess with our financial decisions. But let's break down how this happens and where Maya—and maybe you—can get tripped up.

### FOMO AND SOCIAL PRESSURE

Ah, FOMO—Fear of Missing Out. If there's one thing Maya's

generation deals with daily, it's the constant flood of social media posts reminding her of all the things she's not doing. Whether it's influencers on Instagram showing off their latest gadgets or friends at rooftop parties, Maya's FOMO often leaves her feeling like she's missing out if she doesn't spend.

"I can't tell you how many times I've had to stop myself from buying a plane ticket or a new jacket," she says. "It's like every time I scroll through my feed, someone else is doing something cooler."

**"Kid, there's alw**ays someone doing something cooler. But here's the thing—you've got your own race to run. Don't let someone else's highlight reel make you empty your wallet."

### *STRATEGY: COMBATTING FOMO*

Psychologists suggest practicing mindfulness when FOMO kicks in. Maya learned to pause and ask herself, "Is this something I truly want, or am I just caught up in the moment?" She also started budgeting for the experiences she really values. "I set aside money for fun stuff—brunches, trips, whatever. That way, when I do spend, it feels intentional."

Uncle Aaron puts it simply: "It's like saving for dessert. You don't have to say no to every treat, but make sure it's in the budget before you hit the ice cream shop."

## FINANCIAL ANXIETY AND STUDENT LOAN STRESS

One of Maya's biggest stressors is the weight of her student loans. While she's excited about her career, the monthly loan payments are a reminder of the financial burden she's carrying.

**"Debt's a funny t**hing," Uncle Aaron says. "When you don't have it, you fear it. When you do have it, you ignore it. Either way, it's sitting there, waiting for you to deal with it."

Maya's financial anxiety really hit when she started working full-time. "It's hard to enjoy your success when you're constantly worrying about what you owe," she says.

### STRATEGY: TACKLE DEBT WITH A PLAN

Experts recommend breaking down debt into manageable chunks. Maya started by consolidating her loans, which helped her see the big picture more clearly.

"Once I had everything in one place, I realized it wasn't as overwhelming as I thought," she says. She also started making small extra payments whenever she could, chipping away at the debt faster than she'd expected.

**"Debt's like a wi**ld horse. You've got to rein it in before it runs you over. But once you've got control, you can ride it to the finish line."

## STRESS SPENDING AND EMOTIONAL BUYS

We've all been there—stress spending after a rough day or splurging on something fancy to feel better. For Maya, stress spending often hits when work gets overwhelming. "I tell myself I deserve it, even though I know I probably shouldn't," she admits.

**Uncle Aaron laugh**s, "That's like putting a band-aid on a sinking ship. Feels good for a minute, but it's not going to stop the flood."

### STRATEGY: THE 24-HOUR RULE

To curb emotional spending, Maya started using the 24-hour rule. If she feels the urge to buy something impulsively, she gives herself 24 hours to think it over. "Nine times out of ten, I realize I don't actually need it," she says.

**"Sleep on it, and** you'll see how many things don't seem

worth it the next day."

## DEVELOPING A GROWTH MONEY MINDSET

Now that we've identified the emotional triggers, let's focus on shifting your mindset. This is where the Growth Money Mindset comes into play.

### *SHIFTING FROM SCARCITY TO ABUNDANCE*

Both Maya and Zero know what it's like to operate from a scarcity mindset—feeling like no matter how much you make, it could all disappear. This fear often comes from growing up in times of financial instability or being in debt.

*"I used to think if I didn't take every opportunity that came my way, I'd fall behind,"* Zero says. *"But I learned that not every gig is worth the stress. It's okay to pass on some things and trust the right opportunities will come."*

Maya felt the same. "For a long time, I was too cautious with my money. I was afraid to invest in myself," she says. But eventually, she realized that not every dollar has to be hoarded. "I signed up for a marketing course to sharpen my skills. It cost a bit upfront, but it's already paying off in my career."

### *STRATEGY: VISUALIZATION AND GOAL SETTING*

Both Maya and Zero learned to embrace an abundance mindset—focusing on future opportunities instead of being paralyzed by current limitations. Visualization became a powerful tool for them. Maya visualizes paying off her student loans and being debt-free, while Zero pictures himself running his own photography studio in Miami one day. These long-term goals keep them focused, even when financial stress tries to get in the way.

Maya also found that setting specific, measurable goals helped her shift her mindset. "It wasn't enough to just say 'I want to pay off my debt,'" she explains. "I needed a plan. So, I broke it down—$300 a month toward loans, an extra $50 whenever I can. That way, every payment feels like I'm moving closer to being debt-free."

Zero did the same with his savings goals. "I wanted to upgrade my camera gear, but instead of stressing about it, I set up an automatic savings plan. I put away a little from each gig, and before I knew it, I had enough saved for the gear I wanted—without breaking the bank."

## UNCLE AARON'S TAKEAWAY

Uncle Aaron, of course, has his own version of an abundance mindset. "Back when I was your age, I was always worried about running out of money," he says, laughing. "Now, I've learned that money comes and goes, but opportunities? Those come if you're patient and prepared. Focus on building skills, making smart investments, and letting your money work for you. Trust me, the abundance will follow."

**He pauses, and wi**th a wink, adds: "And if you're ever tempted to splurge? Just make sure it's something that adds value in the long run. Like my self-cleaning lawnmower. Don't judge—it was on sale."

### CASE STUDY:
### *MAYA'S TURNING POINT WITH A FINANCIAL ADVISOR*

MAYA'S FINANCIAL TURNING POINT CAME WHEN SHE FINALLY DECIDED TO MEET WITH A FINANCIAL ADVISOR. NOW, AT FIRST, MAYA WAS HESITANT. "I THOUGHT ONLY PEOPLE WITH A TON OF MONEY USED FINANCIAL ADVISORS," SHE ADMITS. "AND HONESTLY, I WAS KIND OF EMBARRASSED ABOUT MY FINANCES. I FELT LIKE I DIDN'T HAVE IT TOGETHER ENOUGH FOR SOMEONE TO HELP."

BUT AFTER SOME ENCOURAGEMENT FROM UNCLE AARON

(AND A LITTLE RESEARCH), SHE BOOKED A SESSION WITH A FINANCIAL ADVISOR WHO SPECIALIZED IN HELPING YOUNG PROFESSIONALS MANAGE DEBT AND PLAN FOR THE FUTURE. "I WAS NERVOUS AT FIRST, BUT AFTER JUST ONE MEETING, I FELT LIKE I HAD A ROADMAP," SHE SAYS.

THE ADVISOR HELPED MAYA MAP OUT HER FINANCIAL GOALS, BREAKING THEM DOWN INTO ACHIEVABLE STEPS. TOGETHER, THEY CREATED A STRATEGY FOR PAYING OFF HER STUDENT LOANS, BUILDING AN EMERGENCY FUND, AND SETTING ASIDE MONEY FOR FUTURE INVESTMENTS AND LIFESTYLE GOALS.

"WE AUTOMATED MY SAVINGS AND DEBT PAYMENTS," MAYA EXPLAINS. "NOW, A PORTION OF EVERY PAYCHECK GOES STRAIGHT TO MY LOANS AND SAVINGS. IT'S LIKE I DON'T EVEN HAVE TO THINK ABOUT IT. I ALSO SET UP SEPARATE ACCOUNTS—ONE FOR EMERGENCIES AND ANOTHER FOR TRAVEL AND FUN STUFF. THAT WAY, WHEN I SPEND, I KNOW I'M NOT DERAILING MY PROGRESS."

WITHIN SIX MONTHS OF WORKING WITH HER ADVISOR, MAYA HAD NOT ONLY MADE SIGNIFICANT PROGRESS ON HER LOANS, BUT SHE'D ALSO STARTED INVESTING IN A RETIREMENT ACCOUNT—SOMETHING SHE HADN'T EVEN CONSIDERED BEFORE. "I USED TO THINK RETIREMENT WAS SO FAR OFF THAT IT DIDN'T MATTER," SHE SAYS. "BUT NOW, I REALIZE THAT EVEN SMALL CONTRIBUTIONS CAN MAKE A HUGE DIFFERENCE OVER TIME."

## BUILDING STRONG MONEY HABITS

It's one thing to shift your mindset, but it's another to build habits that stick. Maya and Zero both learned that strong money habits are the foundation of financial success.

### *AUTOMATE YOUR SAVINGS AND DEBT PAYMENTS*

One of the easiest ways to stay consistent with your finances is through automation. "Set it and forget it," as Uncle Aaron says.

For Maya, automation has been a game-changer. "Every paycheck, I have a portion that goes straight into my savings account, and another portion that goes toward my student loans. It's like out of sight, out of mind. I don't even miss the money because I never see it."

Zero took a similar approach. *"I automate everything—my savings, my investments, even my bill payments,"* he says. *"That way, I don't have to worry about remembering deadlines or wondering if I'm saving enough. It's all happening in the background."*

Automation helps take the emotion out of saving and paying off debt. Instead of relying on willpower, you set up a system that keeps you on track, no matter what.

*"Automate everything you can,"* he advises. "The fewer decisions you have to make, the less likely you are to let emotions get in the way.

And trust me, once you see that savings account growing without even thinking about it, you'll wonder why you didn't start sooner."

### Set Spending Limits and Track Emotional Spending

Another key to mastering your money mindset is setting spending limits and being mindful of emotional spending.

Maya found that setting monthly spending limits for things like eating out, entertainment, and shopping helped her stay on track. *"I use budgeting apps to track my progress,"* she says. *"If I notice that I'm overspending in one area, I adjust for the next month."*

Tracking emotional spending was another game-changer for her. *"Whenever I feel the urge to splurge, I ask myself why,"* Maya explains. *"Am I stressed? Bored? Or do I really need this?"*

By identifying the root cause of her spending, she's able to make more intentional choices.

Zero had a similar experience. *"As an influencer, there's always pressure to keep up with trends,"* he says. *"But now, I set a budget for 'guilt-free spending'—stuff I want but don't necessarily need. Having that budget gives me permission to enjoy life without feeling guilty."*

**"Budgeting isn't** about saying no to everything fun," Uncle Aaron says. "It's about saying yes—to the right things. Give yourself room to enjoy life, but make sure it's within the limits you set. Your future self will thank you."

### *REFRAME HOW YOU THINK ABOUT SAVING*

For most of us, saving doesn't come with the same dopamine hit as spending. But it's all about how you frame it. Believe it or not, saving can actually trigger the same feel-good chemicals in your brain as spending does. It's just that most of us are wired for instant gratification, which is why saving for the future can feel less rewarding.

Maya reframed how she thought about saving by setting up visual goals. *"I created a vision board for my financial goals,"* she says. *"Whether it's paying off my loans or saving for a big trip, having a visual reminder helps me stay motivated. When I save, I'm not just putting money aside—I'm getting closer to my dream life."*

Zero started doing something similar. *"I created separate savings accounts for my different goals,"* he explains. "One account for my dream studio, one for travel, and one for emergencies. That way, I can see exactly where my money is going, and I get excited every time I hit a milestone."

**"Saving isn't abo**ut deprivation—it's about building the life you want. Think of every dollar you save as a step toward freedom. And if you can't see that freedom yet? Create a picture in your mind (or on a board) of what it looks like. Trust me, it works."

## MASTERING THE MONEY MINDSET

In the end, mastering your money mindset isn't about perfection—it's about progress. Maya and Zero have learned to navigate the emotional roller-coaster of financial stress, FOMO, and anxiety while building habits that set them up for long-term success.

For Maya, it's been about balance—knowing when to save, when to spend, and how to enjoy life without guilt. For Zero, it's been about trusting that his career will continue to grow and that his financial future is secure, even when things get unpredictable.

Your money mindset is like a muscle—the more you work on it, the stronger it gets. Whether you're automating your savings, tackling debt, or learning to combat FOMO, you have the tools to take control of your financial journey. And if Uncle Aaron can teach us anything, it's that a little wisdom (and humor) goes a long way.

## UNCLE AARON'S FINAL TAKEAWAY:

"Your mindset is your moneymaker. If you can train your brain to think about money the right way, there's no limit to what you can achieve. And don't forget, progress is progress—even if it's slow. Keep going, kid."

# 19

## <u>Renting vs. Buying a Home</u>

Alright, folks, let's talk about one of the biggest financial decisions you'll ever make: should you rent or buy a home? Now, before you roll your eyes and think, "Uncle Aaron, I'm still living in my childhood bedroom at 29," let me just say—you're not alone.

Times are tough out there, and rent prices are climbing faster than the cost of that cold brew coffee you can't quit. According to recent data, the average rent for a one-bedroom apartment in the U.S. is around $1,700 a month as of 2023.

If you're in New York or San Francisco, well, good luck paying less than $3,000 for a decent spot. It's no wonder so many people are staying at home longer or squeezing into tiny apartments with three roommates and a cat named Whiskers.

But whether you're fresh out of college or finally thinking about putting down some roots, this chapter is here to help you make sense of whether renting or buying is the right move for you. We'll break down the pros and cons of both, dive into the nitty-gritty of mortgages, down payments, and long-term financial impacts, and figure out what works for your specific situation. So grab a cup of coffee (or hey, maybe a cocktail at this point), and let's get into it.

## RENTING: FLEXIBILITY AND SIMPLICITY

Let's start with renting, because, let's face it—most of us start here. Whether you're moving out of your parents' place at 25 (hey, no shame in that!) or splitting rent with a couple of roommates to afford a place in the city, renting offers flexibility without locking you into a long-term commitment.

### *THE PROS OF RENTING*

**Flexibility:**

Renting is perfect for those who aren't ready to settle down in one place. Maybe you're chasing that dream job across the country, or maybe you just don't know where you want to plant roots yet.

Renting lets you pack up and move when the next opportunity knocks without the hassle of selling a house. Think of it as the commitment-free option—kinda like dating around before you're ready to settle down.

Plus, life is unpredictable, and renting gives you the ability to roll with those changes. Whether you suddenly decide you hate the city and want to move to the mountains, or you find a better job in another state, renting gives you the freedom to adapt to life's twists and turns.

**Fewer Responsibilities:**

Here's the thing—when you rent, most of the major responsibilities are on your landlord. Leaky roof? Call the landlord. Air conditioner on the fritz in the middle of summer? Call the landlord.

Toilet clogged because you accidentally dropped your phone in there? (Yes, this happens more than you think.) Call the landlord.

Renting gives you peace of mind because you're not responsible for costly repairs or regular home maintenance. And trust me, that's a big deal when you're just getting started and don't have the budget for surprise expenses like replacing a broken furnace.

### LOWER UP-FRONT COSTS

Renting generally requires much lower up-front costs compared to buying.

Let's take a look at what you'll need financially to move into a rental:

◊ **Security Deposit:** Most landlords require a security deposit before you move in, usually equal to one month's rent (though some places ask for two). This is your landlord's insurance policy in case you trash the place or decide to turn the living room into a makeshift skate park.

The good news is that if you take care of the place, you get your deposit back when you move out. Uncle Aaron's advice: "Be smart. Don't let your deposit disappear over some scratches on the floor from that time you thought you were a DIY guru."

◊ **First and Last Month's Rent:** In addition to a security deposit, some landlords also ask for first and last month's rent upfront. This means you're forking over two months of rent before you even get the keys. It's a big chunk of cash, so make sure you're prepared.

◊ **Application Fees:** Depending on the market, you might also face application fees just to apply for an apartment. These range anywhere from $25 to $75 and are non-refundable.

If you're applying to multiple places, this can add up quickly.

◊ **Renters Insurance:** Renters insurance is often required by landlords, and it's a smart move even if it isn't. It usually costs about $15 to $30 a month, depending on where you live and what it covers. This will protect your belongings in case of theft, fire, or other disasters.

## THE CONS OF RENTING

### *You're Not Building Equity*

Here's the catch with renting—every rent check you write is money that's gone for good. You're paying for a place to live, but you're not building equity, which is just a fancy way of saying you don't own anything at the end of the day. In the long run, buying a home can be a way to build wealth, while renting is more like paying to borrow space temporarily.

**Think about it like this;** after five years of renting at $1,500 a month, you've spent $90,000—and you have nothing to show for it except for some nice memories and maybe a broken Ikea couch. With a mortgage, at least some of that money is going toward owning a piece of property that could increase in value.

### *Rent Can Increase*

Unlike a fixed mortgage payment, your rent can go up every year. And trust me, it probably will, especially if you live in a hot real estate market or your neighborhood becomes more desirable.

Your landlord has the power to raise your rent, and you're left scrambling to cover the new costs. In some cities, rent hikes can be brutal—think 10% or more in places like Austin or Miami, where rents have soared in recent years. So while renting might feel stable for now, don't count on that rent staying the same.

### *NO CUSTOMIZATION*

Want to paint the walls a bright teal or knock out that awkward wall between the kitchen and living room? Yeah, not in a rental. When you rent, your living space is pretty much stuck the way it is.

You don't have the freedom to remodel or make major changes. So if you're the type who dreams of putting your personal touch on a place, renting might feel limiting.

## BUYING: BUILDING EQUITY AND LONG-TERM INVESTMENT

Now, let's talk about buying a home. It's one of those "adulting" milestones that feels exciting but also slightly terrifying. Don't worry—buying a home can be a great long-term investment if you're in the right financial place to do it.

## THE PROS OF BUYING

### *BUILDING EQUITY*

Here's the biggest advantage to buying a home: you're building equity. Every mortgage payment you make brings you closer to owning more and more of your home. Unlike rent, which disappears into the landlord's pocket, your mortgage payments are like an investment in your future. Over time, your home could increase in value, and you'll benefit when it's time to sell.

Uncle Aaron likes to say, *"Think of owning a home as a forced savings account. Every month, you're socking away a little equity, and when you go to sell, that equity could mean a nice payday."* Of course, home values can fluctuate, but in the long run, real estate has historically appreciated, which makes owning a home a way to build wealth.

### *STABILITY*

With a fixed-rate mortgage, your monthly payments stay the same for the life of the loan (typically 15 or 30 years). This means you won't face those rent hikes we talked about earlier.

While rents might go up 5%, 10%, or even 20% in some places, your mortgage will stay exactly the same. If you plan to stay in your home for a long time, this can provide serious financial stability.

Plus, there's something comforting about knowing you have a permanent place that's truly your own—no more worrying about the landlord selling the building or raising your rent. Stability is especially important if you're planning on starting a family or putting down roots in a community.

### *CUSTOMIZATION*

When you own a home, the sky's the limit when it comes to customization. Want to knock down a wall, add a deck, or turn the basement into a game room? Go for it. You can make your home truly yours, and that's a powerful feeling.

*"I remember the first time I bought a house,"* Uncle Aaron says. *"I knocked out a wall between the kitchen and the living room to make it open-concept. The next week, I installed a deck out back. You couldn't stop me. I was like a DIY hurricane."*

Of course, some projects might require permits, but the point is—you have the freedom to create the home of your dreams without answering to anyone.

## WHAT TO EXPECT FINANCIALLY WHEN BUYING A HOME

Buying a home is a huge financial commitment, and it comes with plenty of up-front and ongoing costs.

Here's a more detailed breakdown of what you can expect when you're ready to make the leap into home ownership:

### DOWN PAYMENT

The down payment is the big hurdle for most first-time home buyers. It's typically between 3% to 20% of the home's purchase price. For example, if you're buying a $300,000 home, that means your down payment will range from $9,000 to $60,000.

The more you put down, the lower your monthly mortgage payment will be. Uncle Aaron's advice: "Start saving early, and don't forget—you'll still need an emergency fund after you make that down payment. Don't throw all your cash into the house."

### CLOSING COSTS

On top of the down payment, there's a bundle of fees known as closing costs, which typically range from 2% to 5% of the home's price. These cover things like title insurance, home inspections, and attorney fees.

For that $300,000 home, you're looking at an extra $6,000 to $15,000 just to finalize the purchase. It's one of those hidden costs of buying that catches people off guard, so make sure you budget for it.

### HOMEOWNERS INSURANCE

Unlike renters insurance, homeowners insurance protects not only your belongings but also the structure of your home. This coverage is typically required by lenders, and costs vary depending on where you live and the size of your home.

On average, you can expect to pay about $1,200 a year for this insurance, though it could be more if you live in an area prone to natural disasters like hurricanes or wildfires.

### PROPERTY TAXES

One of the ongoing costs of owning a home is property taxes. These taxes are based on the assessed value of your home and the local tax rate, and they can vary significantly depending on where you live.

For example, homeowners in New Jersey pay an average of 2.13% of their home's value in property taxes each year, while homeowners in Hawaii pay just 0.31%. Make sure you research the tax rates in your area and factor them into your monthly budget.

### HOMEOWNERS ASSOCIATION (HOA) FEES

If you're buying a condo or a home in a planned community, you might have to pay HOA fees on top of your mortgage. These fees cover the maintenance of common areas, landscaping, and sometimes even things like pools and gyms. The fees can range from $100 to $500 a month, depending on the amenities and the area.

### MAINTENANCE AND REPAIRS

When you own a home, all the repairs are on you. Leaky faucet? Your responsibility. Broken water heater? Time to dip into your savings. Experts recommend setting aside at least 1% of your home's value each year for maintenance and repairs. So, for a $300,000 home, you should budget around $3,000 annually for upkeep.

## THE CONS OF BUYING

### HIGH UP-FRONT COSTS

As you can see from the list above, buying a home isn't cheap. Between the down payment, closing costs, homeowners insurance, and everything else, you're going to need a good chunk of change up-front. If you're not financially ready, home ownership can be a struggle, especially when unexpected repairs or higher-than-expected property taxes hit you out of nowhere.

### *MAINTENANCE COSTS*

Owning a home isn't just about making mortgage payments. You'll also be responsible for maintenance costs—and those can add up fast. Replacing a roof could cost you upwards of $10,000, a new furnace might run $5,000, and even small things like land-scaping and plumbing repairs can start to eat into your budget. So, while home ownership can build wealth, it also comes with financial risks.

**"Owning a home is** kind of like getting a puppy. At first, you're excited, but once the roof leaks or the pipes burst, you realize how much care and attention it really needs. Make sure you're ready for the responsibility."

### *LESS FLEXIBILITY BUYING A HOME TIES YOU DOWN.*

If you want to move for a job or just crave a change of scenery, selling your home can be time-consuming and expensive. You'll need to hire a real estate agent, deal with potential buyers, and hope the market is in your favor. Plus, selling during a downturn could mean losing money, especially if you haven't built up much equity yet.

## MORTGAGES 101:
*How They Work*

Alright, let's talk mortgages—because unless you've got a giant pile of cash lying around, you're going to need a loan to buy a house. A mortgage is a long-term loan that allows you to buy a home, and you agree to pay it back over time, usually 15 to 30 years. The amount you borrow is the principal, and the interest is the cost of borrowing that money.

Here's a quick breakdown of the most common types of mortgages.

## TYPES OF MORTGAGES

### *FIXED-RATE MORTGAGE*

With a fixed-rate mortgage, your interest rate stays the same for the life of the loan, which means your monthly payments won't change. This gives you stability and makes it easier to budget.

Most first-time home buyers go with a fixed-rate mortgage, especially if they plan on staying in the home long-term.

**"A fixed-rate mortgage** is like having a steady, reliable friend. You know exactly what to expect each month, no surprises, no drama."

### *ADJUSTABLE-RATE MORTGAGE (ARM)*

An adjustable-rate mortgage starts with a lower interest rate than a fixed-rate mortgage, but after a few years, the rate can go up or down based on the market. The initial low rate can be appealing, but it's risky because your payments could increase significantly after the adjustment period. If you're planning to sell or refinance in a few years, an ARM might make sense, but be cautious.

**"An ARM is like t**hat unpredictable friend who's fun at first but could become a nightmare when you least expect it."

## INTEREST RATES: WHY THEY MATTER

Interest rates play a massive role in determining how much your mortgage will cost over time. A lower interest rate means lower monthly payments and less interest paid over the life of the loan.

Even a small difference in the interest rate can save—or cost—you thousands of dollars.

For example, on a $300,000 loan with a 3% interest rate, your monthly payment will be about $1,265. But if the interest rate jumps to 4%, that monthly payment increases to $1,432. Over 30 years, that extra 1% could cost you more than $60,000 in additional payments.

**"Always shop around** for the best mortgage rates. Even half a percentage point can make a huge difference in what you pay over 30 years.

Don't just go with the first offer you get—compare rates from different lenders, and make sure you're getting the best deal possible."

## RENTING VS. BUYING: WHAT'S RIGHT FOR YOU?

So, should you rent or buy? That depends on your financial situation, your lifestyle, and your long-term goals. Here are a few questions to ask yourself before making the decision:

### *How Long Do You Plan to Stay?*

If you're planning to live in the same place for at least five years, buying might make sense. It gives you time to build equity and allows you to recoup the up-front costs of buying a home. If you're unsure or know you'll be moving soon, renting is probably the safer bet.

### *Can You Afford the Up-front Costs?*

Buying a home comes with a lot of up-front expenses—down payment, closing costs, home inspections, and more. If you don't have significant savings, renting might be the more affordable option right now. But if you've been saving diligently and are ready for the commitment, buying could be a smart long-term move.

### *Are You Ready for the Responsibility?*

Home ownership comes with a lot of responsibility. From maintenance to property taxes, owning a home requires more effort and financial management than renting. Make sure you're emotionally and financially ready for the commitment before diving in.

## UNCLE AARON'S TAKEAWAY:

There's no one-size-fits-all answer to the rent vs. buy debate. It's all about where you are in life and what makes the most sense for you right now. Renting gives you flexibility, while buying can be a great long-term investment if you're ready for it. Just remember—home ownership isn't the "American Dream" for everyone, and that's okay. The key is making a choice that fits your goals and financial situation.

And when in doubt? Talk to a financial advisor. They can help you crunch the numbers and figure out what works best for your specific situation. Now go forth, my young money padawans, and make those smart financial moves!

# 20

## FINANCIAL FREEDOM
## WHAT YOU SHOULD REALLY BE ASKING

Alright, my friend, let's talk about the Holy Grail of all financial journeys—financial freedom. You've probably heard the phrase thrown around on Instagram, plastered across ads, and hailed by gurus everywhere.

But what does it really mean? Is it retiring at 30? Never working again?

Having a Scrooge McDuck-sized vault of gold coins to dive into? Not quite. In reality, financial freedom is less about swimming in wealth and more about having control over your money so you can live the life you want without constantly stressing about bills or debt.

But here's the kicker—you can't do it alone. Even the best of us need a little help from the pros. Whether it's a Financial Advisor (FA), a Certified Public Accountant (CPA), or a legal expert, building wealth takes teamwork.

This chapter is all about understanding who to call when,

what to ask them, and how to build your dream team to guide you on your path to financial freedom.

## THE MYTH OF THE LONE WOLF INVESTOR

There's a common misconception that if you want to build wealth, you have to do it all by yourself. You might think, "Why would I pay someone to manage my money when I can figure it out on YouTube?" I get it—there's no shortage of personal finance content online, and you could spend hours watching free advice.

**But here's the truth:** just like you wouldn't trust your health to a random stranger with a stethoscope, you shouldn't leave your financial future to chance. Pros exist for a reason—they've been through the fire and can help you avoid rookie mistakes.

## WHY YOU SHOULD WORK WITH A FINANCIAL ADVISOR

Let's start with Financial Advisors (FAs). Think of them as your personal finance coach—they help you set goals, create a plan, and stay accountable. Whether you're fresh out of college, just started a new job, or already thinking about retirement (good on you!), FAs can guide you every step of the way.

### What Does an FA Do?

*A good FA will:*

### 1.  Help You Set Clear Financial Goals

Whether you're saving for a house, planning for retirement, or paying off debt, an FA helps you lay out a realistic roadmap.

### 2.  Create a Personalized Investment Strategy

No, they won't just tell you to throw all your money into the latest stock craze. FAs tailor strategies to your risk tolerance, time-line, and goals.

### 3.  Monitor and Adjust Your Plan

The market's always changing—just like life. An FA keeps an eye on things and makes adjustments when necessary to keep you on track.

### 4.  Be Your Accountability Partner

Having someone check in on your progress ensures that you're sticking to your goals and making informed decisions.

## WHAT YOU SHOULD BE ASKING YOUR FA

Now that you know what FAs do, here's a pro tip: Don't be afraid to ask questions. In fact, the more questions, the better. Here are some things you should ask before hiring an FA:

### 1. What's Your Investment Philosophy?

Every FA has a different approach. Some are more aggressive, while others like to play it safe. Make sure their style aligns with your goals.

### 2. How Are You Compensated?

FAs usually get paid in one of three ways: fee-only, commission-based, or a combination. Fee-only advisors are generally considered more transparent since they're paid directly by you and not by commissions from selling products.

### 3. What's Your Experience With Clients Like Me?

You want someone who's dealt with people in your financial situation—whether that's managing student loans, buying a house, or preparing for retirement.

### 4. How Will You Measure My Success?

Make sure they're not just chasing quick returns but focusing on long-term financial health and growth.

## WHY A CPA CAN BE YOUR FINANCIAL BEST FRIEND

Now let's talk taxes because, like it or not, they're a huge part of your financial life. This is where a Certified Public Accountant (CPA) comes in. A CPA isn't just for tax season—they can be an invaluable part of your year-round financial strategy.

### How a CPA Can Help You

### 1. Tax Planning

CPAs help you understand how much you owe and identify ways to lower your tax burden. They can advise on deductions, credits, and other legal strategies that save you money.

### 2. Navigating Complex Tax Situations

Got side hustles? Freelance gigs? An investment portfolio? The more complicated your financial situation gets, the more you'll need a CPA to help keep things straight.

### 3. Ensuring You Stay Compliant

Nobody wants a surprise letter from the IRS. A CPA makes sure you're following all the rules and avoiding penalties.

### 4. Long-Term Tax Strategy

Tax planning isn't just about this year—it's about making sure you're setting yourself up for long-term success. Whether you're investing, saving for retirement, or running a business, a CPA ensures you're maximizing your after-tax dollars.

### Questions You Should Be Asking Your CPA

Just like with your FA, it's essential to grill your CPA with the right questions:

### 1. How Can I Maximize My Deductions?

Ask your CPA to walk you through potential deductions specific to your situation, like student loan interest, business expenses, or charitable contributions.

## 2. How Should I Structure My Side Hustle Income?

Gig economy jobs complicate taxes, so your CPA can help determine whether it's time to incorporate or stick with self-employment.

## 3. Should I Adjust My Withholding?

Make sure you're not overpaying or underpaying taxes by adjusting your W-4 at work.

## COLLABORATING WITH PROFESSIONALS:
*Teamwork Makes the Dream Work*

The key to financial freedom is collaboration. You don't have to figure it all out on your own, and frankly, you shouldn't.

Working with professionals like FAs and CPAs takes the guesswork out of wealth-building and helps you avoid costly mistakes. These pros can offer insight, structure, and strategies that you might not be aware of.

## FINANCIAL FREEDOM IS A LONG GAME

One of the biggest misconceptions about financial freedom is that it's something you "achieve" by making a single great move, like landing a big investment or getting a raise. But the truth is, financial freedom is a marathon, not a sprint. It's about making small, smart decisions every day that add up over time.

*Uncle Aaron's Three Steps to Financial Freedom*

## 1. Automate Your Savings

Make saving money something that happens without you even thinking about it. Set up automatic transfers into a high-yield savings account or retirement account.

## 2. Diversify Your Income Streams

Don't just rely on one job or one source of income. Create multiple streams—whether it's through investments, side hustles, or real estate.

## 3. Work With the Pros

Hire an FA to keep your investments on track and a CPA to make sure you're not paying more in taxes than you need to. It's worth the money, trust me.

## UNCLE AARON'S FINAL TAKEAWAY

**Here's the thing:** financial freedom isn't just about hitting a magic number in your bank account—it's about having choices. It's the ability to live life on your own terms, pursue your passions, and not worry about whether the electric bill is going to bounce.

But remember, you don't have to do it alone. Building wealth is a team sport, and having the right people in your corner—whether it's an FA, a CPA, or even a lawyer for those complicated estate matters—can make all the difference in the world.

And finally, always, always ask questions. The more you know, the better equipped you'll be to make decisions that lead you to that ultimate goal: financial freedom.

*Now go forth, my savvy money warriors—ask the pros, build your wealth, and live your best life!*

# BONUS CHAPTER 1

## Social Media, Influencers, and Financial Scams

Alright, fam, let's get real about something that's probably sitting in your pocket right now—social media. We live in an age where everyone and their grandma has an Instagram or TikTok account, and while those platforms are great for memes, life hacks, and dance trends, they're also full of something much more dangerous: financial influencers and scams. You've seen them—those flashy ads or influencers standing next to Lamborghinis, showing off stacks of cash, telling you that you, too, can "make six figures" in just 30 days with their "exclusive" method.

Yeah, no. Let me save you some heartache and money right now: if it sounds too good to be true, it probably is. This chapter is all about helping you navigate the murky waters of social media financial advice without getting caught in a scam. Because, trust me, not all "financial influencers" have your best interest at heart.

## THE RISE OF SOCIAL MEDIA INFLUENCERS

Let's break it down—social media influencers are everywhere, and many of them are making bank by telling their followers how to do the same. The problem is, not all advice is good advice. Some influencers actually know what they're talking about, while others are just after your clicks, likes, and, worst of all, your money.

## THE DANGERS OF "GET RICH QUICK" SCHEMES

You've seen the posts: "Invest $1,000 in this secret strategy and become a millionaire!" or "Follow my course and never work again!" These promises are often attached to "get rich quick" schemes, and they're designed to play on your emotions—fear of missing out (FOMO), desperation, or the dream of financial freedom. But here's the hard truth: There are no shortcuts to wealth. Building wealth takes time, discipline, and smart decisions, not quick fixes.

### How to Spot a Scam

So how can you tell the difference between legit advice and a full-blown scam? Here are a few red flags to look out for when scrolling through social media:

### 1. Over-the-Top Promises

If someone is guaranteeing that you'll make a specific amount of money in a short period of time, run. There are no guarantees in investing or business—anyone claiming otherwise is either lying or trying to sell you something shady.

### 2. High-Pressure Tactics

"Sign up NOW or you'll miss out!" Scammers love to put pressure on you to act fast, so you don't have time to think critically or research their claims. If someone's rushing you to buy their course or invest in their product, take a step back. No legit financial opportunity requires you to act without thinking.

### 3. No Verifiable Credentials

Check the background of any influencer or guru. Are they a certified financial planner (CFP)? Do they have a degree in finance or economics? Do they have any real-world experience? If not, why are you trusting them with your financial future?

### 4. Unclear or Vague Explanations

If the influencer can't clearly explain their method or strategy, it's a huge red flag. Legit experts will be transparent about how their approach works. Scammers, on the other hand, will use vague terms or avoid specifics to keep you confused and compliant.

### 5. Paywalls and Upsells

If every piece of "advice" leads to a paid course or an upsell, you might be dealing with a scammer. A real financial advisor or expert won't hold all the good info behind a paywall. Sure, professionals get paid for their work, but they won't string you along with promises only to ask for more cash at every turn.

## THE SOCIAL MEDIA INFLUENCER ECOSYSTEM

Now, don't get me wrong—not all financial influencers are bad. Some are genuinely trying to help people by offering solid advice. But the problem is the influencer economy often blurs the line between real expertise and flashy marketing.

## THE RISE OF "FIN-FLUENCERS"

Financial influencers, or fin-fluencers, have taken over platforms like TikTok, Instagram, and YouTube. They're young, relatable, and often use personal stories to show how they "hacked the system" to achieve financial success. While some are giving good advice (shout out to those who promote budgeting, saving, and investing), others are just trying to grow their follower count at your expense.

**_HOW TO VET INFLUENCERS_**

Before you start implementing the advice of your favorite "finfluencer," here's how to vet them like a pro:

### 1. Do Your Own Research

Just because someone says something is a good investment doesn't mean it is. Take the time to look up any claims they make. Are they recommending a stock? Research that stock. Are they suggesting a specific investment strategy? Look up real-world examples of how it's worked (or hasn't worked).

### 2. Check for Transparency

A legit influencer will be transparent about their successes, failures, and methods. If they're only showing you the wins and none of the losses, they're not telling you the full story. Look for influencers who talk about their mistakes and the lessons they've learned from them.

### 3. Look for Certifications and Credentials

Anyone giving financial advice should be certified or have real experience. Look for influencers who are CFPs (Certified Financial Planners), CPAs (Certified Public Accountants), or who have a degree in finance or a related field.

### 4. Beware of Affiliate Links and Sponsored Posts

While there's nothing inherently wrong with influencers making money from sponsorships or affiliate marketing, it's important to question their motivations. Are they recommending a product because it's good or because they're getting a cut of the sales? Be wary of influencers who push products without clear disclosures.

## PROTECTING YOURSELF FROM FINANCIAL SCAMS

Even if you don't fall for flashy influencers, you still need to be on guard for financial scams. These can show up in your DMs, emails, and even in the comments of social media posts.

### Common Scams to Watch Out For

### 1. Phishing Scams

You might get an email or message from someone pretending to be your bank or a well-known financial institution asking for your personal information. Don't fall for it. Always check the sender's email address and never provide sensitive information through email or DM.

### 2. Ponzi Schemes

These scams involve someone promising high returns with little to no risk. In reality, they're using new investors' money to pay off earlier investors, and the whole thing eventually collapses. If someone promises guaranteed returns, run.

### 3. Pyramid Schemes

In a pyramid scheme, you're encouraged to recruit others to invest money or buy a product, and you get a cut of what they put in. These schemes rely on constant recruitment, and when the new people dry up, the scheme collapses—leaving everyone who bought in late with nothing.

### 4. Fake Investment Opportunities

If someone slides into your DMs with a "great investment opportunity," be skeptical. Real investment opportunities don't come from random strangers on the internet.

## UNCLE AARON'S REAL TALK:
*Don't Chase the Hype*

Let me tell you something, my son Nicolas is always watching these influencers—half listening, of course—thinking they've got all the answers.

**But here's the deal:** money takes time to grow. Whether you're investing in stocks, starting a business, or just saving your paycheck, there's no fast track to wealth that doesn't involve risk. It's a long game, and you need to be patient and strategic.

When I was growing up, there were no influencers *(unless you count the guy at the end of the block who gave stock tips between his conspiracy theories)*. But guess what? The advice remains the same: be smart with your money, do your research, and don't get swayed by people promising you the world.

## UNCLE AARON'S TOP 5 TIPS FOR PROTECTING YOURSELF ONLINE

Here are some of my golden rules for navigating the wild world of social media:

### 1. Trust Your Gut

If something doesn't feel right, it probably isn't. Don't be afraid to walk away from an "opportunity" that sounds too good to be true.

### 2. Keep Your Personal Info on Lock

Never share your banking info, Social Security number, or credit card details with someone online unless you absolutely know who you're dealing with.

### 3. Stick to Reputable Sources

When it comes to financial advice, stick to reputable sources like certified advisors, well-known financial blogs, or books. And hey, if you ever need guidance, your old pal Uncle Aaron is here for you.

### 4. Slow Down

Scammers thrive on urgency. If someone's telling you to act fast, it's usually because they don't want you to think things through. Take your time before making any financial decision.

### 5. Learn from Professionals

If you're serious about building wealth, work with a real professional—like a Financial Advisor (FA) or a CPA. These people have the knowledge and experience to guide you, and they're not going to ask you to invest in shady pyramid schemes.

## UNCLE AARON'S FINAL THOUGHTS

Look, I get it. The internet is full of people selling dreams, and it's easy to get swept up in the hype. But the truth is, real wealth takes time to build, and the people who are really successful aren't the ones making a quick buck—they're the ones who have a plan, stick to it, and work with the right people.

So, before you click "follow" on that next influencer promising to make you a millionaire by Tuesday, ask yourself: are they selling advice or selling a dream?

Stay smart, stay skeptical, and stay on your path to financial freedom. And remember, your money journey is yours—not someone else's Instagram highlight reel.

Now, go forth and scroll wisely!

# BONUS CHAPTER 2:

## NEGOTIATING FOR FINANCIAL SUCCESS

Alright, folks, let's talk about something that might make some of you cringe: negotiation. Yep, that thing we all dread but absolutely need to master if we want to win at the money game. Now, before you start imagining high-pressure boardrooms and tense standoffs, let me break it down Uncle Aaron-style: negotiating is just about asking for what you deserve—and making sure you're not getting the short end of the stick.

Negotiation is one of the most underutilized financial tools out there. Whether you're haggling over your phone bill, negotiating a raise, or trying to get a better deal on rent, these strategies can save you thousands over time.

The problem is, too many people are afraid to negotiate. But here's a little secret: everything is negotiable if you know how to ask.

So buckle up, because in this chapter, we're going to break down some killer strategies to make sure you're always coming out ahead when it's time to talk numbers.

And don't worry—we'll keep it fun.

## WHY NEGOTIATION IS KEY TO FINANCIAL SUCCESS

Negotiation isn't just for bigwigs in suits or smooth-talking salespeople—it's for everyone. I don't care if you're negotiating a salary bump at your first job or trying to get your landlord to stop hiking the rent, knowing how to negotiate can literally put more money in your pocket.

**Think about it:** When was the last time you just accepted the first price someone offered you? If it was yesterday, you're leaving money on the table. Whether it's your cable bill or your paycheck, you have more power than you think. The trick is to ask, and ask the right way.

### *Uncle Aaron's Negotiation Mantra:*

**"Closed mouths do**n't get fed." If you don't ask for better, don't expect anyone to give it to you. That's a rule for life and money.

## THE BASICS OF NEGOTIATION: CONFIDENCE IS KING

Now, the first rule of negotiation is confidence. You've got to walk in like you know your worth—even if, on the inside, you're sweating bullets. It's kind of like pretending you're a pro at a game even when you're still figuring out the rules. That confidence can take you far.

**Here's a little trick:** prepare like a boss. Whether you're negotiating a raise or a better price on your car insurance, research is your best friend. Know what others are paying for the same service or what the average salary is for your role.

### *Strategy 1: The Power of Silence*

You know that awkward silence that sometimes happens in conversations? In negotiation, awkward silence is your best friend. When you make your ask—whether it's for more money, a lower bill, or a better deal—don't rush to fill the silence. Let it linger.

**Here's the psychology:** People don't like silence, and they're more likely to fill it by either agreeing with you or offering a better deal.

**Example:**

**You:** *"I've been a loyal customer for years. I'd like to get a better rate on my internet bill."*

**Rep:** Pauses

**You:** Silence

**Rep:** *"Well, let me see what I can do... looks like we can reduce your bill by $20 a month."*

Boom! Just saved yourself $240 a year.

### STRATEGY 2: RESEARCH BEFORE YOU REACH

Before you even think about negotiating, you've got to do your homework. Whether you're dealing with a new job offer or renewing your lease, you need to know what a fair deal looks like.

For example, if you're negotiating salary, find out what others in your industry are making. Websites like Glassdoor or Payscale can help you figure out the going rate for your job. If you're haggling on rent, look at what other apartments in your area are going for. The more info you have, the stronger your position.

**Example:**

Before you go to your boss to ask for a raise, find out the average salary for your role in your location. That way, when you ask, you're not just pulling numbers out of thin air. You're armed with data, which makes you look more legit.

### STRATEGY 3: USE THE "IF-THEN" TECHNIQUE

This one's a personal favorite of mine because it's basically playing chess while everyone else is playing checkers. It's all about giving options: "If you can do this, then I can do that."

**Example:**

**You:** *"If you can bring my rent down by $100, then I'll sign a two-year lease instead of a one-year lease."*

**Landlord:** Thinks *"Deal."*

Now, they get security, and you get a better price.

This method is great because it creates a win-win situation.

You're not just demanding something—you're offering something in return. It shows you're willing to work with them, which makes it harder for them to say no.

### STRATEGY 4: THE BUNDLE DEAL

Sometimes you can get the best deal by bundling. This works for everything from your cable bill to insurance. Companies love it when you use multiple services because it keeps you loyal to them. Use this to your advantage.

**Example:**

**You:** *"I'm currently paying for car insurance and renters insurance with you. What kind of deal can you give me if I add life insurance to the package?"*

**Insurance Rep:** *"Let me see... looks like I can knock $150 off *your annual premium if you bundle."*

Who doesn't love getting more for less? Plus, bundling usually simplifies your billing, which is always a win.

### STRATEGY 5: NEGOTIATE YOUR BILLS

Did you know that bills are negotiable? Most people think that when a bill shows up in the mail or inbox, that's the final price. But here's the deal: most service providers—whether it's internet, phone, or utilities—have wiggle room, especially if they know you're about to walk away.

**Example:**

**You:** *"Hey, my phone bill keeps going up. I've been a loyal customer for three years, but I'm seeing better rates with other providers. Can we talk about a lower plan for my current usage?"*

**Customer Service Rep:** *"Let me check what promotions we have available for long-term customers."*

Boom, you just scored a discount without switching companies.

### STRATEGY 6: NEGOTIATE YOUR RENT

Rent is often the biggest chunk of a young adult's budget. But just because it's set by a landlord doesn't mean it's set in stone. There are always ways to negotiate, whether it's through a discount for renewing your lease or bartering for repairs or improvements.

**Example:**

**You:** *"I'm considering staying another year, but I noticed the rent is going up by $100. Would you be willing to keep it the same if I commit to a two-year lease?"*

**Landlord:** *"Hmm, that sounds fair. Let's do it."*

Rent negotiations are all about timing and loyalty. If you've been a good tenant (paid on time, no complaints), your landlord will likely want to keep you rather than find a new tenant.

### *Strategy 7: Salary Negotiation*

You knew this was coming, right? Salary negotiation is probably the most important negotiation you'll ever do because it compounds over time. A $5,000 bump at 25 can turn into hundreds of thousands by the time you retire.

**Here's how to do it:**

**1. Know Your Worth:**

Do the research. Understand what your role pays in your area. Armed with data, you can confidently ask for a number that's reasonable and fair.

**2. Frame it with Value:**

Don't just ask for more money. Explain why you deserve it. Highlight what you've accomplished in the past year or how you've grown in your role.

**Example:**

**You:** *"I've been with the company for two years and have consistently exceeded my sales targets. Based on my contributions and market research, I believe a salary adjustment to $70,000 would reflect my value to the team."*

**3. Be Ready for a Counteroffer:**

Sometimes they'll meet you halfway. If you were asking for $70,000, they might offer $65,000. Decide ahead of time what your bottom line is, and be willing to negotiate benefits, vacation time, or bonuses if the salary number isn't exactly what you wanted.

## UNCLE AARON'S FINAL THOUGHTS ON NEGOTIATION

**Here's the bottom line:** Negotiation isn't about being greedy—it's about making sure you get what you're worth. Whether it's your salary, your rent, or even your phone bill, you owe it to yourself to ask for more.

Because guess what?

No one's going to give it to you if you don't ask.

**Remember this:** The worst thing they can say is no. And even then, you've lost nothing.

But if they say yes?

You've just scored yourself a better deal, more money, or less stress. That's a win in my book. So go out there and negotiate like a boss—because you've got nothing to lose and everything to gain.

# APPENDIX: TOOLS, RESOURCES, AND HELPFUL EXTRAS

This appendix is your go-to section for all the tools, resources, and cheat sheets you'll need as you start applying the lessons from Uncle Aaron's Money Adventure.

Whether you're looking for a budget template, need to find the right app for tracking your side hustle income, or just want to double-check a financial term, this section has you covered.

## BUDGETING AND FINANCIAL TRACKING TOOLS

These are some of the best apps and websites to help you stay on top of your finances. Uncle Aaron-approved, of course.

### 1. Mint

**Platform:** Web, iOS, Android

**What it does:** Tracks your income, expenses, savings goals, and even your credit score all in one place.

**Why Uncle Aaron loves it:** It's free, and it gives you a clear picture of where every dollar goes. No more guessing about where your money disappeared to.

### 2. YNAB (You Need A Budget)

**Platform:** Web, iOS, Android

**What it does:** Helps you create a proactive budget by giving every dollar a job.

**Why Uncle Aaron loves it:** YNAB's method is all about planning for the future, not just tracking what you've already spent.

### 3. Personal Capital

**Platform:** Web, iOS, Android

**What it does:** Combines budgeting with investment tracking. Great for seeing your entire financial picture.

**Why Uncle Aaron loves it:** It's especially useful for tracking your net worth and seeing how your retirement savings are doing.

## SIDE HUSTLE AND FREELANCE TOOLS

Starting a side hustle or managing freelance work? These tools will help you organize your projects, track income, and stay on top of your taxes.

### 1. QuickBooks Self-Employed

**Platform:** Web, iOS, Android

**What it does:** Tracks income and expenses, separates personal and business transactions, and helps with quarterly taxes.

**Why Uncle Aaron loves it:** Great for freelancers who want to keep their financial life organized without having to hire an accountant.

### 2. FreshBooks

**Platform:** Web, iOS, Android

**What it does:** Invoicing, time tracking, and expense tracking for freelancers and small business owners.

**Why Uncle Aaron loves it:** Simple invoicing features make it easy to get paid faster.

### 3. Wave

**Platform:** Web

**What it does:** Free invoicing and accounting software.

**Why Uncle Aaron loves it:** It's completely free and perfect for small businesses and side hustlers just starting out.

## INVESTING RESOURCES

Ready to start growing your money? These platforms will help you get started with investing, no matter your experience level.

### 1. Vanguard

**Platform:** Web, iOS, Android

**What it does:** One of the largest investment platforms, great for opening IRAs and investing in index funds.

**Why Uncle Aaron loves it:** Low fees and a wide range of index funds make this a great choice for beginners looking to build long-term wealth.

### 2. Robinhood

**Platform:** Web, iOS, Android

**What it does:** Commission-free trading for stocks, ETFs, and cryptocurrencies.

**Why Uncle Aaron loves it:** Easy-to-use interface for new investors who want to dip their toes into the market without paying fees.

**3. Betterment**

**Platform:** Web, iOS, Android

**What it does:** Automated investing with a focus on long-term goals like retirement.

**Why Uncle Aaron loves it:** Betterment takes the guesswork out of investing by automatically managing your portfolio based on your goals.

## INSURANCE RESOURCES

Insurance can feel overwhelming, but these tools will help you compare policies and find the best coverage for your needs.

**1. Policygenius**

**Platform:** Web

**What it does:** Compare quotes for life insurance, health insurance, renters insurance, and more.

**Why Uncle Aaron loves it:** It's a one-stop shop for comparing policies, and it makes buying insurance a lot less confusing.

**2. Lemonade**

**Platform:** Web, iOS, Android

**What it does:** Affordable and easy-to-use renters and homeowners insurance.

**Why Uncle Aaron loves it:** Simple, affordable, and you can get a policy in minutes.

## CREDIT SCORE TOOLS

Your credit score is important, and these tools will help you keep tabs on it.

### 1. Credit Karma

**Platform:** Web, iOS, Android

**What it does:** Free credit score tracking and credit monitoring.

**Why Uncle Aaron loves it:** It's free, easy to use, and even offers tips for improving your score.

### 2. Experian

**Platform:** Web, iOS, Android

**What it does:** Provides your Experian credit report and score for free.

**Why Uncle Aaron loves it:** You can see what's affecting your score and even dispute errors directly through the platform.

## TAX TOOLS

Whether you're a side hustler or just starting out, filing taxes can be confusing. These tools will make tax season a little less painful.

### 1. TurboTax

**Platform:** Web, iOS, Android

**What it does:** Guides you through filing your taxes step by step.

**Why Uncle Aaron loves it:** It's user-friendly, and you can file both simple and complex taxes easily.

### 2. H&R Block

**Platform:** Web, iOS, Android

**What it does:** Online tax filing with the option to get help from a real tax professional.

**Why Uncle Aaron loves it:** A great option for those who want a little extra help with their taxes.

## BOOK RECOMMENDATIONS

### 1. "I Will Teach You to Be Rich" by Ramit Sethi

*Why Uncle Aaron Recommends It:* A no-nonsense guide to managing money, this book is full of practical advice on saving, investing, and living a rich life—without pinching every penny.

### 2. "The Simple Path to Wealth" by JL Collins

*Why Uncle Aaron Recommends It:* Perfect for beginners, this book teaches you the power of index funds and simple, effective investing strategies that anyone can follow.

# Financial Terms Glossary

Here's your go-to glossary for all the financial terms used throughout Uncle Aaron's Money Adventure. Whether you're just starting out or brushing up on your money knowledge, this glossary will help you understand the key concepts we've covered in the book.

## 401(K)

A retirement savings plan offered by many employers that allows employees to save and invest for retirement on a tax-deferred basis. Contributions are made from your paycheck before taxes, which lowers your taxable income. Some employers offer matching contributions.

## 403(B)

A retirement savings plan for employees of public schools and tax-exempt organizations. Like a 401(k), contributions are tax-deferred.

## 529 PLAN

A savings plan designed to encourage saving for future education costs. It offers tax-free growth and tax-free withdrawals when used for qualified education expenses.

## APR (ANNUAL PERCENTAGE RATE)

The total annual cost of borrowing money, including interest and any fees, expressed as a percentage. It's how much you'll pay on credit cards, loans, or mortgages over a year.

## ASSET ALLOCATION

The strategy of dividing your investments across different asset categories like stocks, bonds, and real estate to reduce risk.

## CAPITAL GAINS

The profit made from selling an asset like stocks or real estate for more than you paid for it. Capital gains are subject to taxes.

## COMPOUND INTEREST

Interest calculated on the initial principal, which also includes all of the accumulated interest from previous periods. Compound interest allows your money to grow exponentially over time.

## CREDIT SCORE

A numerical representation of your creditworthiness, based on your credit history. Scores range from 300 to 850, with higher scores indicating better creditworthiness.

## CRYPTOCURRENCY

A type of digital or virtual currency that uses cryptography for security. Bitcoin is the most well-known example. It operates on decentralized networks and is independent of traditional banking systems.

## DIVERSIFICATION

A risk management strategy that involves spreading your investments across different asset types (e.g., stocks, bonds, real estate) to reduce risk.

## DIVIDEND

A portion of a company's earnings paid to shareholders, typically in cash or additional shares of stock.

## EMERGENCY FUND

Money set aside to cover unexpected expenses or financial emergencies, like car repairs or medical bills. The standard recommendation is to have 3-6 months of living expenses saved.

## ESTATE PLANNING

The process of arranging for the management and disposal of your estate after death. This includes wills, trusts, and other legal documents to ensure your assets are distributed according to your wishes.

## FICO SCORE

The most widely used credit score in the U.S., ranging from 300 to 850. It's used by lenders to evaluate your creditworthiness.

## FIRE (FINANCIAL INDEPENDENCE, RETIRE EARLY)

A movement that encourages extreme saving and investing to allow individuals to retire much earlier than traditional retirement age.

## HIGH-YIELD SAVINGS ACCOUNT

A savings account that pays a higher interest rate than a standard savings account, allowing your money to grow faster.

## INDEX FUND

A type of mutual fund or ETF (exchange-traded fund) designed to track the performance of a specific market index, like the S&P 500. Index funds are popular because they are low-cost and diversified.

## INFLATION

The rate at which the general level of prices for goods and services rises, decreasing the purchasing power of money over time.

## IRA (INDIVIDUAL RETIREMENT ACCOUNT)

A tax-advantaged account designed to help individuals save for retirement. There are two main types: Traditional IRAs (contributions are tax-deductible, but withdrawals are taxed) and Roth IRAs (contributions are made with after-tax dollars, but withdrawals in retirement are tax-free).

## IUL (INDEXED UNIVERSAL LIFE INSURANCE)

A type of permanent life insurance that offers both a death benefit and a cash value component. The cash value grows based on the performance of a stock market index, such as the S&P 500.

## LIABILITY INSURANCE

A type of insurance that protects you from financial losses if you're responsible for injuring someone or damaging their property.

## MUTUAL FUND

An investment vehicle that pools money from many investors to purchase a diversified portfolio of stocks, bonds, or other securities.

## NET WORTH

The total value of all your assets (e.g., cash, investments, property) minus all your liabilities (debts). It's a snapshot of your financial health.

## PASSIVE INCOME

Money earned with little to no effort on your part. Examples include rental income, dividends, and royalties.

## PREMIUM

The amount you pay for insurance, usually on a monthly or annual basis, to maintain your coverage.

## PRINCIPAL

The original amount of money invested or borrowed, before any interest or returns.

## REBALANCING

The process of adjusting your investment portfolio back to its original asset allocation to maintain your desired risk level.

## ROTH IRA

A type of IRA where contributions are made with after-tax income, but the money grows tax-free and withdrawals in retirement are also tax-free.

## S&P 500

An index that tracks the 500 largest publicly traded companies in the U.S. It's often used as a benchmark for the overall stock market.

## STUDENT LOAN FORGIVENESS

Programs that cancel all or part of a student loan debt for eligible borrowers, typically based on their profession (e.g., teachers, public service workers) or meeting specific conditions.

## TERM LIFE INSURANCE

A type of life insurance that provides coverage for a specific period (term). If the insured dies during the term, the policy pays a death benefit to the beneficiaries.

## TRUST

A legal entity created to hold assets for the benefit of certain persons or entities. Trusts are commonly used in estate planning to manage wealth for future generations.

## UNDERWRITING

The process by which an insurance company evaluates the risk of insuring a person or asset and determines the terms of the policy, including the premium.

## WHOLE LIFE INSURANCE

A type of permanent life insurance that provides coverage for the insured's entire lifetime. It also has a cash value component that grows over time, which can be borrowed against or withdrawn.

**This glossary is** designed to be a handy reference as you navigate your financial journey. Keep it nearby, and don't hesitate to revisit it whenever you need a refresher on a term or concept. Remember, understanding the language of money is a powerful tool in mastering your financial future!

# CONCLUSION:

# YOU'VE GOT THIS, NOW LET'S GET MOVING!

Alright, folks, if you've made it this far, first of all—congratulations! You've stuck through all the talk about budgeting, saving, investing, insurance, and everything in between. I know it can feel like a lot, but trust me, you're already miles ahead of where I was when I started my financial journey. Whether you're here to get out of debt, save for something big, or just take control of your financial future, you've got everything you need to make it happen.

But before we wrap this up, let's take a moment to step back and look at the big picture. This book has been full of advice, personal stories, and steps to follow—but none of it matters unless you take action. And here's the thing: You don't have to be perfect. You just have to get started.

### THE JOURNEY OF A THOUSAND BUCKS BEGINS WITH ONE DOLLAR

Let's face it: getting control of your finances can feel overwhelming. There's so much to think about—so many steps to take—that it's easy to get stuck before you even start. You might be thinking, "I'll wait until I've got more money," or "I'll budget when things settle down." But here's the truth: there's never a perfect time. You don't need a big windfall or a perfect set of circumstances to get started.

You can start small—like really small. In fact, that's often the best way to begin. Have a few bucks left over at the end of the week? Save them. Got a part-time gig? Set aside a tiny percentage of it for an emergency fund. The beauty of this journey is that every little bit helps, and over time, all those small steps add up to big wins.

### UNCLE AARON'S FIRST SMALL WIN

Let me tell you a story—this one's a little more uplifting than my infamous $400 pizza debacle. I was about 25, working my first real job after leaving the Marines. I wasn't rolling in money, but I was managing to pay my bills and have a little fun on the side. Now, back then, I wasn't exactly what you'd call financially savvy. I didn't have a budget. I didn't have a savings account. I was living paycheck to paycheck, and I thought that was just how life worked.

Then one day, I decided to try something new. I had $50 left over at the end of the month—not a fortune, but more than I usually had. Instead of blowing it on a night out or a new gadget, I did something radical: I put it in a savings account. Just $50, sitting there in the bank.

I can't lie to you—it wasn't a life-changing amount of money, but it was symbolic. It was the first time I ever chose to save instead of spend. That $50 turned into $100 the next month, then $200 after that. Before I knew it, I had a small emergency fund, and suddenly, I didn't feel so stressed about money all the time. It wasn't because I was rich—I wasn't—but because I had started to take control.

That's the power of small steps. No matter how little you start with, those tiny decisions create momentum, and before you know it, you're moving in the right direction.

## RECAPPING WHAT YOU'VE LEARNED: BUILDING BLOCKS FOR SUCCESS

Let's break down some of the key points we've covered throughout this book. If you remember nothing else, let these principles be your foundation moving forward.

### *Budgeting is Your Roadmap*

Budgeting isn't about restricting your spending or living like a hermit. It's about giving your money a purpose. When you tell your dollars where to go, you're less likely to wonder where they went. A solid budget doesn't just help you cover your bills—it makes room for the things you enjoy (fun money!), all while preparing you for the future.

### *Saving is Non-Negotiable*

Whether it's $5 or $500, saving is essential. Emergencies will happen, and opportunities will arise. Having a financial cushion lets you handle the unexpected without sinking into debt, and it gives you the freedom to say "yes" to the things that matter most. The sooner you start, the better, because compound interest is your best financial friend. It turns small, consistent savings into something bigger over time.

### *Invest Early, Invest Often*

If there's one thing we've learned, it's that time is the most important factor when it comes to investing. You don't need a lot of money to start—just time and patience. The earlier you begin, the more time your money has to grow.

Whether it's index funds, stocks, or even crypto, the key is to diversify your investments and let them work for you over the long haul.

### *Insurance Protects You From Life's Curveballs*

Health insurance, car insurance, and other forms of coverage aren't just necessary evils—they're lifesavers when life throws you a curveball. The last thing you want is to get hit with a massive bill because you thought you didn't need coverage. Trust me, it's worth paying those premiums up-front to avoid financial disaster down the road.

### *Debt Doesn't Have to Control You*

Debt is part of life for most of us, but it doesn't have to be a permanent burden. There are ways to pay it off—whether it's the snowball method, the avalanche method, or just tackling it one step at a time. The key is to make a plan, stay disciplined, and avoid letting high-interest debt linger. The faster you eliminate debt, the more money you can put toward your future.

### *What I Want You to Remember:*
*Financial Success is in Your Hands*

Here's the most important takeaway: You are in control. You have the power to shape your financial future. It doesn't matter where you're starting from, how much debt you have, or how little you've saved up so far.

What matters is that you take that first step, and then another, and another. This journey is about progress, not perfection.

I know it can be scary to look at your financial situation and feel overwhelmed. I've been there—I've made mistakes, taken detours, and learned the hard way.

But the best part about managing your money is that you can

always course correct. The key is to stay focused on your goals, learn from your setbacks, and keep moving forward.

### *Uncle Aaron's Final Story:*
*The Power of Consistency*

One last story before I let you go. Back when I first started investing, I didn't know much about the stock market. I had a few friends who were way more into it than I was, and they were always giving me advice—some good, some not-so-good. I wasn't in the game for a big win; I just wanted to grow my money slowly and steadily.

So, I started small, putting $50 a month into an index fund. Nothing fancy, just consistent investing. I'll admit, there were months when I was tempted to pull that money out and spend it on something more fun, but I stayed the course. And you know what happened? Over time, that little $50 a month turned into something substantial.

It wasn't flashy, but it worked. That's the lesson here: consistency beats flashiness every time. Whether you're saving, budgeting, or investing, staying consistent is what leads to success.

## UNCLE AARON'S ACTION PLAN:

**1. Start Small:** Don't wait for the perfect moment or the perfect amount of money. Whether it's $5 or $50, start saving and investing today.

**2. Automate Your Finances:** Set up automatic transfers to your savings and investment accounts so you don't even have to think about it. Automation takes the guesswork out of financial success.

**3. Create a Realistic Budget:** Make a budget that fits your life, not someone else's. Be honest with your income and expenses, and don't forget to include a little fun money to keep things balanced.

4.  **Review and Adjust Regularly:** Life changes, and so should your financial plan. Set aside time each month to review your budget, savings, and investments. If something isn't working, adjust it.

5.  **Get Insured:** Don't skip the important stuff like health insurance or car insurance. A small premium now can save you from financial disaster later.

6.  **Tackle Debt:** If you're in debt, make a plan to pay it off. Start with the highest interest debt first or tackle the smallest balance to build momentum—just start somewhere.

7.  **Stay Consistent:** This is the big one. Financial success doesn't happen overnight. It's about making small, consistent decisions that add up over time. Stick with it, and you'll see results.

## FINAL THOUGHTS: IT'S TIME TO TAKE ACTION

Now that we've covered the basics—and some of the advanced stuff—you're ready to tackle your financial future head-on. Remember, this isn't about becoming an overnight millionaire (though hey, if that happens, congrats!). It's about taking control of your money, setting yourself up for success, and giving yourself the freedom to live the life you want.

You've got this. I know you do. And if there's ever a day when it feels like too much, just think back to Uncle Aaron's $50 savings story or that fateful $400 pizza. I made the mistakes so you don't have to. You're already ahead of the game just by reading this book, and now it's time to put what you've learned into action.

*Go forth, budget, save, invest, and insure like a pro. Your future self will thank you.*

# EXPLORE SELF HELP TITLES

Take a journey through collection of self-help books, where life's challenges are met with wisdom, humor, and practical advice.

Each title is designed to empower and guide readers through various aspects of personal and professional growth:

◊ Bounce Back: Resilience for Life's Curveballs
Discover practical strategies for building resilience and facing life's unexpected challenges head-on, helping you grow stronger from adversity.

◊ Adulting Guide: Failing, Learning, and Thriving
Navigate the complexities of adulthood with real-life lessons, humorous anecdotes, and practical advice to help you thrive through challenges and failures.

◊ **The Entrepreneur's Playbook:** Strategies for Success
Equip yourself with actionable insights and strategies for entrepreneurship, covering everything from market
research to leadership and creating a lasting legacy.

With decades of experience across various fields, self-help books combine relatable stories, hard-earned wisdom, and practical steps to empower your personal and professional journey.

# Author Bio

**Aaron B. Kershaw** is an author, mentor, and former U.S. Marine whose mission is to empower others through resilience, financial education, and practical life skills. With a diverse career spanning corporate leadership, media production, and community service, Aaron combines humor, insight, and hard-earned wisdom in his writing.

His early experience managing a business as a high school student laid the groundwork for a lifelong dedication to helping others, a path that led him to significant roles with organizations like Habitat for Humanity and Guiding Eyes for the Blind.

A licensed financial advisor, insurance professional, and educator, Aaron has guided individuals and businesses through complex financial landscapes, helping them make informed decisions and reach their goals.

Known for his straightforward and relatable approach, he focuses on making life's toughest concepts more accessible and actionable. Beyond business and self-help, Aaron also writes teen thrillers, captivating younger audiences with suspenseful, action-packed stories.

Through his books, Aaron inspires readers of all ages to navigate life's unexpected twists, grow from every setback, and build a life of resilience and purpose.